RED HOT MONOGAMY

IN JUST 60 SECONDS A DAY

BY
PATRICK T. HUNT, M.D.

CCC PUBLICATION • LOS ANGELES

Published by

CCC Publications
21630 Lassen Street
Chatsworth, CA 91311

Manufactured in the United States of America

Cover © 1994 CCC Publications

Interior layout & production by Oasis Graphics

ISBN: 0-918259-53-3

If your local U.S. bookstore is out of stock, copies of this book may be obtained by mailing check or money order
for $6.95 per book (plus $2.50 to cover postage and handling) to: CCC Publications; 21630 Lassen St.; Chatsworth, CA 91311.

Pre-publication Edition – 5/94

DEDICATION

To my wife,
Denise,
and the product of
Red Hot Monogamy,
our new
son.

WARNING!

Overuse of these powerful methods of communication can result in extreme fatigue, structural damage to your bed, and a chronic smile on your face that only a plastic surgeon can remove.

Table of Contents

HOW TO USE THIS BOOK

1. Read the whole book first.

The book is divided into three main sections. In part I, we'll look at how and why the fireworks fizzled. Part II details the powerful techniques you can use to rekindle the passion and restart the fire in your lover's pants. You'll learn exactly the WHAT, WHERE, WHEN, WHY, HOW, and just as important, what NOT to do to re-ignite your romance. In Part III we'll tie all the techniques together and shows you how to apply them on a daily basis.

2. Pay particular attention to the chapter called, "A DAY IN THE LIFE OF A RED HOT LOVER."

This chapter demonstrates how to consolidate and combine the Red Hot Lover techniques detailed in part II of this book in a practical, real world situation. There will be a second by second accounting so that the reader can see exactly how, in just sixty seconds a day, he or she can make love last a lifetime.

3. Go back and reread the RED HOT REVIEWS.

These concise summaries at the end of most chapters will allow you to refresh your memory in the future without rereading the whole text. Note also that these pages are highlighted so you can flip through the book and easily locate them. To keep track of the specific techniques, you may also want to make wallet size flash cards to carry with you.

4. Use the RED HOT MONOGAMY CHECKLIST discussed in the last chapter.

This five point checklist is the "Core Curriculum" of all Red Hot Lovers and should be used every day.

PART

I

CHAPTER 1

HEAVEN ON EARTH

Since you've purchased this book, I assume that you are in a monogamous relationship with someone very special to you. And I know it has been somewhat of a quest to find them.

LADIES, you went on that herb and onion diet, sweated to the oldies, and listened to a thousand stupid opening lines from jerks during happy hour.

MEN, I'm sure you sat through countless boring dinners and maybe you even took a chance on those "sure thing" blind dates, not to mention wading through those stuffy cocktail parties, the church bingo picnics, and garden club mixers, hoping to find your dream girl. Yes, but now it's all worth it. You'd gladly do it all again because now you've found...

THE LOVE OF YOUR LIFE!

Or maybe you didn't date. You were afraid to. You're shy and reserved - still hoping to win the Lottery of Love. Waiting for Kismet... Fate...the Winds of Chance with a little help from Cupid, to throw you and your soul mate together. Whatever circuitous path you took, finally, one day it happened.

LADIES, you finally met the man of your dreams - your own Prince Charming and Adonis rolled into one tight, little package. So handsome, women swoon when he walks by; so modest, he doesn't even notice. In fact, all Mr. Perfect sees is you. He's devoted, caring, and compassionate. He has a job with a future and flosses his teeth after every meal. Why, he even rewinds every video he rents.

MEN, you too could tell immediately you were smitten on that first date when she took her napkin and wiped that smudge of chocolate pudding off your cheek. She was the paragon of beauty, grace, and style...so considerate that she exhales CO_2 onto her plants so they can breathe easier.

Life couldn't be better. Traffic lights turn green on your approach. You have the power to shake exactly two aspirin out of the bottle. The guy at McDonalds gives you extra ketchup packets without being asked. And you're having great sex - morning, noon, and night.

Oh yes, life is wonderful, isn't it? You're on top of the world. It's great, it's wonderful, it's...

HEAVEN ON EARTH!

You are sure you're going to be in love with this person forever, or until at least the universe implodes.

You become an item. For some of you, the rest follows rather quickly. Those long weekends together. Quiet whispers of "I love you" in front of the fireplace. You spend so much time with one another that you decide to move in together. There's talk about commitment and...VOILA! In the twinkle of a diamond, you prance, trot, or gallop down the altar.

"Marry me and I'll never look at another horse"
                    Groucho Marx in <u>*A Day at the Races*</u>

The honeymoon in Cancun goes so fast. Writing the thank you notes. Getting the new nest in order. Back to the old grind. Time flies. Then it happens. It sneaks up on you. At first you don't believe it. But one day you wake up and realize...

CHAPTER 2

THE GOOSE BUMPS DON'T LAST FOREVER

It can be subtle at first. Tiny things creep up. Little hints that the magic is gone. Things unnoticed in the passion of night come into a sharper focus in the light of day.

LADIES, can his breath, once as fresh as the morning dew, now take the curl out of your perm? Does the man you once thought could give Einstein a run for the money say he won't eat snails because the only likes fast food?

MEN, are those once charming little quirks in HER personality - like yelling "Bingo" when she has an orgasm - beginning to get just a little bit old?

YES! YES! YES!...you say?

Women can tell very quickly things are not going to work out - it's almost instinctive with them. For men, it's a little harder. So, guys, I've included a few of the more subtle indicators for you.

TOP TEN SUBTLE CLUES THAT SHE MAY **NOT** BE THE GIRL OF YOUR DREAMS:

1. She uses CB lingo when you make love.
2. Thighs rubbing together in corduroy pants causes smoke detectors to go off.

3. Blames her mood swings on solar flares.
4. Used to work with Donkey in Tijuana strip joint.
5. Can eat her own weight in McNuggets.
6. Talks loudly in restaurant about her yeast infection.
7. Uses raw veal to soothe flaming hemorrhoids.
8. Red rash on inner thigh turns out to be ringworm.
9. Wants to go to France so she can stand in line to watch old Jerry Lewis movies.
10. Has a nickname for each of her veneral warts.

Then it gets...WORSE.

The blindness of infatuation becomes a 20/20 nightmare. The forest fire of passion becomes barely a pilot light. The fireworks fizzle. The hurricane of passion turns into a drizzle.

It may take years, months, days, or perhaps minutes for some of you. Don't feel bad. It happens to the best of us. We're creatures of habit. We tie our shoes the same way every day, sleep on the same side of the bed and drive the same way to work.

And when things become habitual, we take them for granted. Familiarity breeds boredom. It's HUMAN NATURE.

Sure, the magic may return for a fleeting moment or two, but the spark of passion is gone.

IT'S NEVER NIRVANA.

You already know every story, antidote, every joke your lover can tell. You've fondled every fold and ogled every orifice.

These couples are everywhere. But it seems a great concentration of them can be found in fine restaurants. The next time you bop down to your local bistro, glance around the room. You don't have to be a psychologist to guess who the married ones are. They're staring blankly into space. Eyes glazed over. In a word...

BORED!!!

Not all, but a lot of them. All they have to look forward to is the duck a l'orange. Even if you're not married, a lot of you in serious relationships have experienced the same thing.

Losing the magic is not just a matter of being bored. With ortho-dontia bills, second mortgages, and two-hour commutes taking their toll, it's no wonder you have less time for bedroom romps.

THE NUMBER ONE REASON FOR A DWINDLING SEX LIFE IS JOB RELATED STRESS.

With the compressed lifestyle that many of you follow, you probably don't have time to floss your teeth, let alone be romantic.

Not only are some of you missing out on great sex, you're probably arguing with your lover on a daily basis. You soon meet boredom's cousins, irritation and resentment. You find yourselves nagging back and forth, caught in a labyrinth of complaints and counterattacks.

> *"My wife and I were happy for twenty years. Then we met.*
> **Rodney Dangerfield**

You know what follows. The bedpartners of boredom and a decreased sex life are adultery and divorce.

DIVORCE COURT

Here come some frightening statistics. More than 50 % OF MARRIAGES END IN DIVORCE. Repeat offenders do even worse, with 60% of second, 70% of third, and 80% of fourth marriages ending in divorce court.

The same holds true for serious relationships. The more times you "go steady" (or, for the more politically correct, "undertake psycho-physical pair bonding and checking account conjoining"), the more likely you are to break up. Part of the reason for this is...

MOST COUPLES SPEND MORE TIME PLANNING THEIR WEDDING THAN THEY DO WORKING ON THEIR MARRIAGE.

> *"Always get married early in the morning. That way, if it doesn't work out, you haven't wasted a whole day."*
>
> **Mickey Rooney**

The statistics on divorce are sobering. There is obviously a lot of unhappy people out there. Even if you're one of the lucky 50 percent that stay married for a year or more.

ONLY ONE OUT OF NINE MARRIAGES LASTS TEN YEARS.

WHEN TO RAISE THE WHITE FLAG

Let's save some time here. It may be pointless for some of you to continue in your marriage. But how do you know? When is it time to throw in the towel? Not an easy decision. And as especially diffcult one for us men who are by nature, fixers. We never like to admit defeat.

For just this reason, I've included the following guidelines...

MEN's TOP 10 GROUNDS FOR DIVORCE

1. Her stretch marks show up on Satellite recon photos.
2. She has ticks in pubic hairs the size of jelly beans
3. Before her period she blows up like an inflatable life raft
4. Universe expands at same rate as her stomach.
5. Calls her sex organ "Senor Itchy."
6. She has orgasm watching Hulk Hogan body slam the Macho Man.
7. You find out her former lovers include carnival geek and Ernest Borgnine.
8. She keeps frozen spit collection in ice box.
9. Her favorite pastime is chewing on barbequed badger testes.
10. Hairs stuck to deodorant stick turn out to be pubic.

If you're picked one of the above, consider the possiblity of divorce. If you're picked two or more, call a divorce attorney immediately. If all ten are true, skip the court date and consider a six week course of EST (electroshock therapy).

THE LUCKY HALF

Let's say you're one of the lucky - depending how you look at it - 50% that stays married. The bad news is that seven out of ten married men have affairs! And three out of ten married women have affairs. Some recent studies even suggest that our better halves, especially professional or career women, are equaling the male statistics for double dipping. Obviously, there's a serious problem here with home cooking. And one, hopefully, that *Red Hot Monogamy* can fix.

Before we continue, you **MEN** should know that women seem to feel, and perhaps rightly so, that you just aren't as romantic, considerate, and attentive as you were on the first date. What happened to that **RED HOT LOVER**? Here's a little test to see just how bad things are...

LADIES, PICK THE STATEMENT OR STATEMENTS THAT YOU MOST OFTEN SAY TO YOUR LOVER:

a. "You never open the car door for me anymore."
b. "Ouch! Just don't jam it in."
c. "Why can't we kiss more?"
d. "Why do I always have to give *you* head?"
e. "Do you always have to watch TV while we're doing it?"

If you picked ONE of the above, consider yourself average.

If you picked TWO of the above, you *might* have a problem.

If you picked ALL of the above, you *do* have a problem. Keep reading and in the meantime, hide the TV remote.

CHAPTER 3

WHAT YOUR LOVER NEEDS MORE THAN ANYTHING

The KEY to this book, to making the person you love happy, to having a great relationship AND great sex is to...

MAKE YOUR LOVER FEEL SPECIAL!!!

It's the ultimate aphrodisiac. This is what women and men want more than anything. Everything that follows is, in one way or another, tied in to making the person you love feel wanted, needed, sexy, and desirable. How you make a person feel when they're around you is the key.

They have to feel that you appreciate what they do for you and who they are. And you must give her or him this love, respect, recognition, and admiration...EACH and EVERY DAY. They want to feel that they MATTER to you more than anything else in the world. That they have made you happy and that your life would be INCOMPLETE without them.

They want their needs to be considered above all others; they want to be NUMBER ONE, your first priority. They want you to be PROUD of them and secure in the knowledge that they are your PRIME consideration in life.

The rest of this book is geared to showing you in detailed fashion how to do just this - and have FUN doing it. It's easier than you think and it's only going to take SIXTY SECONDS a day!

THE SECRET IS IN THE PAST

The SECRET to a happy relationship is always in the PAST. At some earlier point in your relationship you and your lover were residents of Cloud 9. What things did you do that triggered romantic feelings?

Obviously, if you want to feel that way again, start doing whatever it was that worked before. And avoid the things that made you sad or angry. It's that simple. After years of corrosion of a relationship, its just hard to pry those feelings loose. It's hard to steer out of the ruts of complacency. You may feel silly, vulnerable, stupid. That's okay. Remember that, especially in a D.O.A. relationship, YOU have to take the first step.

The Red Hot Monogamy method takes a COGNITIVE approach to relationships. What this basically means it that you CONCENTRATE on the THINGS THAT WORK instead of spending all your time analyzing what went wrong.

BUILD ON YOUR STRENGTHS RATHER THAN DISSECT YOUR WEAKNESSES.

Don't dwell on the negatives. Forget past failures. Don't be a whiner or finger pointer. Leave that dirty laundry in the hamper. Focus on you and your lover's strengths, not your weaknesses.

THE BUTTERFLY EFFECT

The reason the techniques in this book work so well is based on a little known phenomena called the BUTTERFLY EFFECT.

Noted meteorologist, Dr. E. Lorenz, found that minute changes have profound effects on complex systems like weather. He described this as the Butterfly Effect because, as he put it, a butterfly flapping its wings in Brazil might create a tornado in Texas. What this means to you is that a small effort can cause a big change in your relationship. By investing as little as a minute, you CAN markedly change things for the better. And your sex life will be fantastic. GUARANTEED!

Why? Let me tell you a SECRET that all great lovers and sexual experts know...

GREAT SEX STARTS IN THE HEAD, NOT THE BED!

If you want to know how good a couple's love life is, just watch how much they talk to one another. To get your message of caring, concern, and compassion across to that someone special, you have to know how to communicate. Ergo...

GREAT COMMUNICATION IS THE KEY TO GREAT SEX!

Communicating well is one of the most important life skills you develop.

GREAT COMMUNICATION IS THE KEY TO GREAT RELATIONSHIPS!

"What we've got here is a failure to communicate."
Strother Martin in <u>Cool Hand Luke</u>

A man or woman who takes time to talk with his lover has a responsive mate. And as you will see, if you want PASSION BETWEEN THE SHEETS, you will have to learn to fulfill his or her needs OUTSIDE the bedroom.

GETTING WHAT *YOU WANT* OUT OF THE RELATIONSHIP

The best way of getting your lover (or people in general) to do what *you* want is an art.

TO THE DEGREE YOU GIVE OTHERS WHAT THEY WANT, THEY WILL GIVE YOU WHAT YOU WANT.

It seems incredibly simple but few people really understand it. The secret is that YOU must FIRST give your lover what they want. Then they will give you what you want.

Most people have it backwards. A husband says to himself, "I would give my wife some flowers it she would show me more affection." A wife crackles, "I could be a lot more romantic towards Harold if he wasn't so cold and crabby."

They both have the formula backwards - the man has to bring his lover flowers first, then he'll get the affection. She has to warm up to Harold first; then the indiffecence and grumpiness of Harold will melt away. So that's that way the principle works. You *first* give your lover what they want; then they in turn give you what you want. This is the SECRET of RED HOT MONAGOMY.

Of course it takes patience. And a few other things. You also have to know what the other person wants. And knowing how to give them what they want. And knowing what it is you want and what you're willing to give to get it.

CHANGE "WANT" TO "NEED"

You may want to consider one modification of this formula. Replace the word "want" with "need." "Wants" are frivolous, itchy, plundering, often greedy forces that are never satisfied - fill one want and two more take its place. "Needs" are the deeper currents of one's existence. They are worthy and meaningful - not as capricious as "wants."

People *want* riches - they *need* fulfillment.

People *want* fame - they *need* recognition.

People *want* sex - they *need* love and perhaps a little of all of the above.

Thus Red Hot Monogamy is not about GETTING; it's about GIVING. And loving. And succeeding. In fact, it's about becoming immensely successful. For it you can get things done with people in harmony, help them grow and achieve their goals and become more than they were before, then you are a special person that possesses a treasured talent.

The good news, as you will soon see, is that it can be done in only SIXTY SECONDS A DAY!

PART

II

CHAPTER 4

THINGS YOU SAY

This is a rather broad category but the underlying principle is rather straightforward...

EVERY DAY GIVE YOUR LOVER A HUG WRAPPED IN A WORD.

Pamper them with pronouns, assure them with adjectives, and validate your love for them with verbs.

1. <u>NOTICE THEM</u>

At various times in our lives, we all feel put upon and underappreciated or taken for granted - that our mate doesn't notice us or really care that much about how we look or even feel.

To be a Red Hot Lover, you must NOTICE your lover. If you only do one thing after reading this book, THIS SHOULD BE IT!!!

MEN, if she's sporting a new spring ensemble, tell her how attractive the pastel colors look on her. Comment on how delicious dinner was last night even if it was Spam and cucumber sandwiches. When she comes home from aerobics, tell her how great she looks. Pinch her tush, explaining that it looked so cute you couldn't help yourself. In short,

LET HER KNOW HOW SPECIAL SHE IS!

WOMEN, if you don't know this already, let me tell you one of the biggest secrets for happy relationship...

ALL MEN ARE SUCKERS FOR COMPLIMENTS.

Tell the man you love at least once a day how special he is to you. Tell him how SEXY he looks taking a shower. Let him know you APPRECIATE and are CONSCIOUS of how hard he works for you. If he keeps the checkbook, let him know how you could never keep all those numbers straight and what a good job he does at it. Comment how nice the car looks after he waxes it. Pay attention to what he does.

LET HIM KNOW THAT WHAT HE DOES MATTERS!

2. GIVE GOOD COMPLIMENT

The secret to giving good compliment is to be SPECIFIC. Try to tie it in with your lover's habits or hobbies. Make it personal. This takes a little practice.

MEN,

— **Don't Say,** "Thanks. Dinner was good."

— **Do Say,** "That crab rangoon was incredible. And that mu goo sauce was orgasmic. Really delicious. Almost as delicious as...you."

— **Don't Say,** "You look nice".

— **Do Say,** "Is that outfit new? That plaid skirt really brings out the color in your eyes. You look stunning. But I think it's going to look even better laying on the chair next to the bed."

PRAISING YOUR LOVER IN FRONT OF YOUR FRIENDS MULTIPLIES THE EFFECT OF A COMPLIMENT MANY TIMES OVER.

They may blush a little but everybody loves it.

The impact also is greatly increased by TIMING. Surprise her when she least expects it. Whisper to your wife how much you love a certain part of her anatomy as you stand in line at the grocery store. At a cocktail party mumble in her ear how sexy her legs look in those black hose.

Whenever she has done something, if you can't think of anything witty or creative, *just say something nice.*

SAYING NOTHING WILL BE TAKEN AS DISAPPROVAL

Maybe even as an insult.

LADIES, the same applies to you. Whisper in his ear how cute his behind looks in those new jean shorts when you're at the Jaycee picnic. Compliment him on his quality that you admire. Thank him for noticing the thing *you* do. Let him know how *boring* life would be without him. Tell him how proud you are of him for being so successful.

COMPLIMENT YOUR LOVER AT LEAST ONCE A DAY.

Try to reinforce your lover's ego, polish their self-image to a bright luster. Make them feel good about themselves and they'll make you feel good in return. Investing a little ten second compliment will pay back hours, perhaps days, of your partner - and you - feeling warm, wanted, and wonderful.

However, don't over do it. Everybody is hip to phony compliments. It's like the movie reviewer who always says, "IT'S A 10!" After a while, it loses its impact. Be sincere but not obsequious. Feed your lover a steady diet of baloney and you'll both wind up with a stomach ache.

RED HOT WARNING!

FIVE STAR BUTT KISSING WILL GET YOU DEMOTED TO A PRIVATE AS QUICK AS YOU CAN SAY "SCHWARTZKOFF."

---

3. LEARN HOW TO TAKE A COMPLIMENT

This is not as easy as it sounds for many people, including yours truly. What you SHOULD do is simply accept your lover's praise. DON'T DISAGREE OR BE CRITICAL OF YOURSELF! When HE tells you that you look nice, don't mutter, "My hair's a mess!" When SHE comments how good you look in your suit, don't reply, "These pants are too tight. I'm such a fat slob." Instead reply, "I'm glad you think so" or "Thanks for noticing."

4. SWEET GREETINGS

Greet your lover every morning with a smile. Ask them how they slept. Say "good-bye" or "I love you" when the two of you part.

If your LOVER calls you in the middle of a hectic day and you can't talk, don't utter, "What a F___ing day this has been! Gezus Christ what do YOU want?" This is an extreme example but many of us are prophets of gloom and doom, almost NEVER having a good day.

Even if the alligators are biting your toes, take just a moment to give your spouse a pleasant hello or a "I miss you, honey," before you tell them you're tied up but you'll call them back. And thank them for calling before you hang up.

And at the end of the day, be enthusiastic about being reunited your lover. Our bloodhound, Henry, jumps up and down, tailing waging, barking, licking, and drooling all over me. And he does this EVERY time I come home.

For us humans, a greeting consisting of a "HI" and a KISS is sufficient - save the drueling for special occasions. Throw in an occasional hug, squeeze, and a smile for good measure.

Even if your day has been a catastrophe, don't let it interfere with your time at home. It's like the old story that if you had two glasses of milk, one sour, the other fine. Why pour the sour into the fresh and wreck them both? Don't let disappointments at work sabotage your home life. Leave all the negatives at the office.

5. <u>THE RIGHT WAY TO ASK FOR SEX</u>

You've heard the thunder and its time for lightning to strike. First of all, if you use the techniques in this book, in no time at all, you won't ever have to ask. But for those times when you want to communicate to your lover that you're looking forward to the "wild thing", I have a few suggestions.

MEN, instead of saying something like, "Do you wanna do it or not?"BE CREATIVE.   SUGGEST to your lover that you'd like to make love, use a lighter approach...

<u>TOP 10 SYNONYMS FOR "69":</u>

1. Oral Gonad Hockey

2. Slurping down Mayor McCheese's Secret Sauce

3. Frosting the Pastry

4. Smoking Pickles

5. Tongue surfing on the Bald Hermit

6. Priming the Porridge Pump

7. Arresting the Bearded Outlaw

8. Blowing the Meat Whistle

9. Syphoning the Python

10. Preflight the Pocket Rocket

<u>RED HOT WARNING!</u>

MEN...THERE'S A FINE LINE WITH GOING OVERBOARD WITH YOUR MONIKERS. I STRONGLY SUGGEST AVOIDING PHRASES SUCH AS, "I WANT MY KNOB SLOBBED" OR "HEY YOU WHORE BANDIT, BE MY SUCK SLAVE."

Even though there are over 500 synonyms in the English language to describe the penis, most women won't come right out and tell a man they want to grab it.

Words like "DICK," "PRICK," and "COCK" are too vulgar, too "hard," for many women to use (except in moments of extreme passion).

Just for you LADIES, I've listed below my TOP TEN "SOFT" SYNONYMS for MALE HARDNESS , a.k.a...

TEN WAYS TO SAY "PENIS" WITHOUT GIGGLING.

1. Willy Banana

2. Beef Bayonet

3. Ice Cream Maker

4. Mutton Dagger

5. Pajama Python

6. Dart of Love

7. Mr. Potato Finger

8. Bacon Roll

9. Mr. Stiffy (or at other times, Mr. Wiggly)

10. The Pink Oboe

The neat thing about a penis is you can call it just about anything if you put either "love," "pink," or "big" in front of it - he'll know what you're talking about. LADIES, tell him to give you the "Big Chop Stick," "Pink Buick," or "Love Bulldozer" and I'm sure he'll respond with more than a smile.

6. UNEXPECTED PHRASES OF PASSION

In the middle of a movie, at a P.T.A. meeting, for no particular reason, whisper to your lover, "I LOVE YOU." These are three of the most powerful words in the English language. And don't be afraid to say "ILY" in front of others, ESPECIALLY IN FRONT OF YOUR LOVER'S FRIENDS. And the MORE UNLIKELY THE LOCATION, the GREATER the effect. This is also true of pillow talk.

Don't limit naughty verbs and scintillating nouns to the bedroom. Call your lover during the day when you know they can't respond freely and tell them what you're going to do to them tonight. **MEN**, tell her it's "Big Mac" calling and whisper, "Hold my lettuce, hold my buns, let my pickle have some fun." **LADIES**, call your man at work and order carry out..."I'd like to order a side of thighs. And be sure to bring that secret sauce."

You don't even have to use words. It's amazing how you can carry on a conversation without saying a word. A well-timed sexy grunt or whispered groan in you lover's ear during a lull at the philharmonic concert will have them asking for encores later. Personalize your own favorites and use them on your lover when they least expect it.

7. CAPTAIN KANGAROOS

"THANK YOU." So simple yet so neglected.

MEN, thank HER for every dinner. For caring. For putting up with you, washing your socks, and cleaning the house. For keeping the checkbook balanced and folding your underwear so neatly. Thank HER for giving up "Murphy Brown" so you could watch Monday Night Football.

LADIES, thank HIM for taking the kids to the scouts last night and for helping you stick to your diet. For triming his nasal hair. And especially for installing that air bag in your headboard.

Score an extra 100 points for thanking your lover the next day for a great night of love-making.

The "PLEASE" word is also very powerful. Using it is part of the bigger picture of showing RESPECT for your lover. Even if you've been together for years, POLITENESS counts a lot. **LADIES**, ask him, "Honey, could you PLEASE get me another Diet Coke while you're up?" **MEN,** ask her "Sugarbutt, could you PLEASE pick up a case of Curex for me on your way home?"

MUTUAL RESPECT is one of the KEY ELEMENTS of successful relationships. Be polite to the one you love. Sadly...

OFTEN WE'RE MORE COURTEOUS TO A STRANGER THAN WE ARE TO OUR OWN MATE.

8. THE PERFECT DAY

Ask your lover what their perfect day would be for them. Maybe it's getting up early and running ten miles. Of course, it's just a warm-up for you because you're twenty pounds lighter.

You have breakfast on the veranda of your open air studio in Maui and spend the rest of your day writing another best selling novel.

Share your thoughts, your dreams and aspirations. I find couples are often very surprised when they hear what their partner's idea of their perfect day is.

RED HOT WARNING!

MEN, BE DISCRETE HERE. IF YOUR PERFECT DAY STARTS OUT WITH YOU WAKING UP IN MAUI WITH KIM BASSINGER GIVING YOU ORAL SEX, IT'S PROBABLY BEST NOT TO BE TOTALLY HONEST HERE.

---

9. INTRODUCING YOUR LOVER IN PUBLIC

Let's imagine you two are at some type of social function - PTA mixer, Garden Club Social, Cocktails at the CEO's house - and your lover doesn't know a lot of the guests. Here's your chance to score "mucho" brownie points when you introduce your mate.

MEN,

Don't Say, "Oh, and this is my wife."

Do Say, "Here's my best pal and the sexiest woman in the city."

Also good are, "I'd like you to meet...the love of my life," "the best thing that ever happened to me," or "the woman who puts the roll in my toostie." Hold her hand as you do. Put your arm around her. Give her a peck on the cheek.

LADIES,

Don't Say, "Here's my old man."

Do Say, "Here's the man who puts the pepperoni in my pizza."

Other expressions to try for you ladies are, "Meet the world's greatest bandit...he stole the stars from the sky and put them in my eyes." Or try my favorite, "Meet Mr. Red Hot Monogamy..."

RED HOT WARNING!
DON'T EVER RUN YOUR LOVER DOWN IN FRONT OF YOUR FRIENDS. *DO* NOT CHIDE YOUR LOVER OR MAKE FUN OF HIM OR HER. DO AND YOU'LL SEE YOUR RELATIONSHIP - AND YOUR SEX LIFE - GO INTO THE DEEP FREEZE.

---

10. SECRET CODES and STRANGE PERSONAS

Make up your own language to talk about things. Nicknames for one another or for having sex. The old standards are "snooker dumpling," "baby sweet cakes," or "making whoopee."

MEN, try giving your fave female a male nickname like "FRED" or "GEORGE." I don't know why, but women get a kick out of this. Make up a code expression for having sex like "SHAKING HANDS WITH PRESIDENT JOHNSON", "JUMPING INTO THE LOVE BUNKER," or "PICNIC ON THE GRASS." They can be as obscure as you like - "FEEDING THE RACOON" or "PARKING THE WINNEBAGO."

LADIES, start calling your lover "HOMO BIGGEST ERECTUS." (loosely translated from the Latin, it means "LARGE AND HARD.") Another pet moniker to try is "P.O.P." - "PREFERRED ORGASM PROVIDER." I would avoid nicknames such as "BOTTOM FEEDER" or "BLOOD-SUCKING HEARTWORM."

Another thing to try is to call your lover in the middle of the day. Only it's not going to be you calling...exactly. You can make up your own cast of goofy characters. **MEN**, try to disguise your voice and act like "Momar," that famous Middle East therapist with the distinctive lisp, the man whose hands are registered sexual weapons, who's calling to remind her of your special appointment that evening.

Or be "Julius Scissor" and tell her about the special trim work you specialize in.

LADIES, if you do reach your lover during the day, you still can play like you're someone else. Be MISSION CONTROL at the Kennedy Space center and tell him about how you're looking forward to the space shuttle "Trojan" attempting re-entry tonight.

RED HOT REVIEW
"THINGS YOU SAY"

1. **NOTICE THEM.**
   Silence will be construed as disapproval.

2. **GIVE GOOD COMPLIMENT AT LEAST ONCE A DAY.**
   Personalized compliments in front of their friends multiply the effectiness.

3. **LEARN HOW TO TAKE A COMPLIMENT.**
   Don't disagree or be self-critical.

4. **SWEET GREETINGS.**
   Always take time to say hello and good-bye.

5. **THE RIGHT WAY TO ASK FOR SEX.**
   Suggest rather than demand. Be creative and use a little humor.

6. **UNEXPECTED PHRASES OF PASSION SCORE BIG.**
   The more unlikely the location or time, the greater the effect, especially in front of your lover's friends.

7. **DON'T FORGET THOSE CAPTAIN KANGAROOS.**
   "Please" and "Thank You" are very powerful words. They show you notice and you care.

8. **FIND OUT WHAT YOUR LOVER'S PERFECT DAY IS.**
   Sharing your dreams and aspirations is important, and you'll often learn something about your partner you never knew.

9. **INTRODUCE YOUR LOVE IN PUBLIC WITH PRAISE AND PIZAZZ.**
   These public displays of affection score mucho brownie points.

10. **DEVELOP YOUR OWN SECRET CODE WORDS, PHRASES, AND PERSONAS.**
    Pet monikers and nicknames for sex engender closeness and playfulness in a relationship.

CHAPTER 5

THINGS YOU DO

This category could fill two books with all the possibilities. I've assembled the most important ones for you to try. The common thread in all of what follows is, whatever you DO, make sure they're things that make your lover feel very special, deeply loved, and totally irreplaceable.

1. TRADING PLACES

Show that you appreciate your mate's responsibilities and chores by doing them for a day.

MEN, some weekend, YOU be Mr. Mom. Try waxing the floor and cleaning out the cat litter box. Making the bed and vacuuming the house. Scrubbing the skid marks off the toilet bowel and picking up your own clothes. While you're doing this, tell her to get out of the house - go shopping or play cards with her friends. And instruct her NOT to return before six P.M. She'll come back all smiles and you'll have a fresh perspective on what her life is like.

The all-time best, BROWNIE POINT MOVE (BPM) for men is to come home early and FIX DINNER for you lover. It doesn't matter if the steak is overcooked and the asparagus is soggy. She'll love you for trying.

"When Sears comes out with a riding vacuum cleaner, then I'll clean the house."

Roseanne Arnold

LADIES, the same goes for you. Try cutting the grass or taking out the trash. Paying the monthly bills and balancing the checkbook. The exact "chore" you do will obviously vary from couple to couple. Score extra points by doing something he particularly dreads doing.

2. OPEN UP THE COMPLAINT DEPARTMENT

At least twice a year some quiet night when things otherwise seem calm take out some three by five cards and both of you make out a list of "THREE THINGS YOU DO THAT BOTHER ME."

MEN, you will be amazed at the things you didn't even realize you do that bother her. Maybe it's those clothes you throw on the floor. Or the fact that you never tell her "thanks" for dinner. Or that you never kiss her before or during sex. Or that she really doesn't like the smell of your farts.

You **LADIES** might also not realize how much your talking to him before dinner while he's trying to read the paper bothers him. Maybe he just wants some "P & Q" after a long day at work. If this is the case, give him some decompression time where you leave him alone.

When you see this list...

DON'T GET YOUR FEELINGS HURT.

Most of us counterattack when criticized - or we deny it. That's human nature. Instead of retaliating with a nuclear strike on your partner, try saying, "I didn't know I was doing that." Or, "I'm willing to work on that."

Consider the following story about Ted and Mary. Whenever they got in the car, Ted always changed the radio station to a Country and Western station. One night as they were driving home from their twentieth wedding anniversary party, Mary told him, after enduring this for years, that she was saying good-bye to Conway Twitty and changed the station.

Expecting the worst, she was totally flabbergasted when her husband let out a big sigh and thanked her for being so thoughtful on this special day. He admitted that he, in fact, HATED Country and Western music and was only trying to be NICE to her by tuning in that station. Equally surprised, she admitted that the only reason that she listened to it was because she thought that HE liked it.

The same story applies to the woman who always gave her husband the yolk of the egg and ate the white herself. For twenty years this went on. Only after he had a heart attack from all that cholesterol did he finally discover that his wife was only being nice to him - she thought he wanted the yolk while in fact SHE loved it.

The tragedy here is that these couples didn't communicate about what they liked and disliked and thus wound up being miserable.

3. TAKE AN INTEREST IN YOUR LOVER'S LIFE

This means getting involved in both their day to day duties around the house as well as any hobbies or intersets he or she may have.

MEN, let's assume your special someone loves to work in the garden. She gets excited over tulip bulbs. Watching plants grow is not your idea of fun. You might get excited over two lips but only when they're on your bulb.

What does a RED HOT LOVER do? Go out and pull some weeds. (She'll wind up pulling you later.) You don't have to spend hours doing this, just make an effort.

LADIES, say he's into power tools. He's got saber saws, grinders, every screwdriver Sears makes and loves to fix things. Only you wish he'd spend more time on you instead of the toaster. Does he spend hours playing flight simulator games on his computer? Don't be jealous. Try taking an interest and be his copilot once in a while. Don't ignore his hobbies. Embrace them. If he nearly has an orgasm watching Hulk Hogan body slam the Macho Man, sometimes you'll just have to go with it.

4. <u>GET OUT OF THAT RUT</u>

Humans are creatures of habit. It's the brain's way of economizing thought so we don't have to think about the small stuff. We brush our hair a certain way, drive to work the same way and take the same chair at the dinner table every night.

So too do we behave in habitual patterns. Most of our interactions are automatic. "Hi. What's new?" The same thing happens in our relationships. And in our sex lives. We go through life on AUTOMATIC PILOT.

BREAK THE PATTERN!

You're in love with ONE person. No variety here. But fill up the rest of your life with variety. Do something different. Try a new restaurant. Take a hike somewhere you've never been. Have sex in some part of your house or apartment you never have before. Go square dancing. Try out that new comedy club. Go to a church of a different faith. Read your lover a bedtime story from a sexy novel.

I'm not saying you've got to go trekking in Nepal, but just do something DIFFERENT. Try getting outside more. Experience nature.

> *You live on a SQUARE street. Work in a SQUARE office. But you've got a ROUND body. Try to get outside once in a while where nothing's square.*

Spend a weekend away. You make all the arrangements. Or even stay in a hotel in town. Hotel rooms do different things to different people. They make me want to take naps and order room service. However, a lot of women get, well, is "aroused" the right word? Maybe "stimulated" or "risqué" is a better choice. It brings out the naughtiness in them, plus it gives them an excuse to try out their latest black lace teddy from Victoria's Secret.

5. <u>PRIME TIME</u>

Sometime during the week, spend some time together without TV. Just the two of you. Take a walk, watch a sunset. It's amazing how little people really talk to one another, especially those with kids. Sweet nothings and passionate somethings are sometimes hard to hear over the sound of alarm clocks, car-pool horns, and crying babies.

> *In his lifetime the average American male spends 24 years sleeping, 10,935 hours reading, and 1.3 years on the toilet.*

Try to make time for the two of you to be alone. Join your two spaces and bond. Share. Exchange. Once a week try to spend at least an hour alone with your lover. Don't worry about the time. I would suggest that you literally take off your watches.

DO SOMETHING TOGETHER!!!

I don't mean going out to eat or to a movie. Joint projects where you work together. Wash your car together. Clean out the garage. Wallpaper the bathroom. Work together and accomplish something. EVEN TRY BEING KIDS TOGETHER.

Blind man's bluff. Tag. Volleyball. Frisbee. Build a sand castle on the beach. Start a snowball fight. Or a bedroom pillow or sock fight. Play Hide and Seek.

6. <u>REACH OUT AND TOUCH SOMEONE</u>

Non-Sexual Touching is very important. Give your partner those hugs, rubs, and tugs. Your lover, just like Labradors and kids, has skin hunger. And you do too. Be generous with the N.S.T. Don't be a person who strokes his pet animal all night long and doesn't even give his lover a kiss goodnight.

In European orphanages during W.W.I, there were "no-touch" policies to prevent the spread of infection. In nine out of ten institutions studied, every baby under the age of two died, despite adequate food and shelter. By the 1940's at Bellevue Hospital in New York City, every baby was picked up and held several times a day. The infant mortality was less than 10 percent. Recent studies showed that infants who were touched for forty five minutes a day gained 47 percent more weight than babies who were not touched.

Every day you should PICK, DIG, SCRATCH, TICKLE, SNIFF, PROBE, FONDLE, RUB, and CARRESS your lover's body, though not necessarily in that order. Women, nuzzle your lover's neck and squeeze his hand. If he gives you a great back rub, leave him a note the next day, "Nice to be Kneaded by You."

"Communication through touch is ten times more effective than by verbal or emotional means."

Steve Canyohn, M.D., Ph.D.

Touch is our primary language. It is the first sense we develop in the womb and our most reliable form of communication in the first years of life.

START PETTING YOUR LOVER ALL NIGHT LONG AND WATCH THEM TURN INTO AN ANIMAL.

7. THE POWER OF A SMILE

Smile at your lover. Smile for no particular reason. It's a very powerful tool. Your lover will probably say something like, "What?" Simply answer, "I was just thinking how lucky I am to be with you." And then they'll smile back at you. Pretty soon you two will be smiling a lot more.

Recent research validates the value of "putting on a happy face." Smiling tightens certain facial muscles which in turn change blood flow patterns. This, in turn, decreases the temperature of the brain's blood supply. Cooler blood in the brain is associated with more pleasant moods, according to Robert Zajonc, Ph.D., professor of psychology at the University of Michigan.

8. <u>DO SOMETHING OUTRAGEOUS</u>

Do something out of the ordinary. Surprise your lover with unexpected behavior. Spice up things with a practical joke. Maybe a singing telegram to his or her office. I'm not suggesting you have to juggle some chain saws - just do *something* out of the ordinary.

LADIES, imagine you're out shopping for a present for your man. No special occasion, except that it was Friday and you're trying to be a RED HOT LOVER. On the clearance rack is, without a doubt, the ugliest orange and green plaid safari shorts you've ever seen this side of a 1975 L.L. Bean catalogue. Grab them! The salesgirl happily sells them to you for three dollars, forcing a smile when she asks if these are a gift. Then buy a real present, like an oversized gray sweatshirt your lover had his eye on. Have them both wrapped up.

Hide the second package containing the sweatshirt. As he excitedly opens the first package, make a big deal out of this neat present you found for him - how it was rather expensive but nothing's too good for him and how you drove all over town to find his size. Watch him disguise a grimace under a smile. Then give him his real present.

MEN, on the way to the concert, act for a second like you forgot the tickets. Or that you forgot to make reservations at the restaurant where there is always a two-hour wait.

LADIES, when he comes home some night, be hiding. Jump out and scare him when he discovers your hiding place. MEN, after she snuggles in bed and the lights are out, go the the restroom and come back as Norman Bates looking for his mother. Or be Dr. Hannibal Lector looking for a bedtime snack.

MEN, try this. Some quiet evening when watching TV, flip to MTV. When a song with a rocking beat comes on, nonchalantly stand up like you're going to the ice box. Slip off your pants, then jump back in front of her and do your best immitation of a Chippendale dancer. Women should try this too.

One point comes to mind here. Some of you may be more of a parent ID or mindset rather than a child ID. You're serious as serious can be. As such, doing the bump and grind in your BVD's may be hard for you to pull off.

Also, with seriously corrorated relationships, this kind of behavior is probably unimaginable. You would feel stupid. Ask yourself why would you. A major part of the reason is that you're making yourself VULNERABLE.

You're setting yourself up for rejection by your mate for your actions, afraid that he or she will think you a complete childish idiot. And they'd be right. That's the SECRET, you see. I want you to PLAY and forget about your bank account and the greenhouse effect and what other people think about you. Being vulnerable, exposing your feelings, and being playful - these are the FIRST 3 STEPS on the road to Red Hot Monogamy AND to enjoying your own life more.

9. SPRING A SURPRISE

LADIES, set up a fishing trip, golf game, or tennis clinic weekend for your favorite Hunkoramus, or maybe a weekend at a health spa or tennis clinic.

MEN, sometime when you're driving, ask her if she could flip down her sun visor. It's even better if it's at night or on a cloudy day. She'll probably question you why. Just tell her the light is reflecting in your eye. Have a rose hidden between the visor with a note saying something like, "From your favorite Red Hot Lover."

Women love surprises. Give your lover a surprise birthday party. Spring a bounce back weekend trip on them. Buy her a day of BEAUTY MAKE-OVER with a pedicure, facial, hair styling, and nails. For the more unfortunate of us, consider adding hair waxing, tooth enamel bonding, and global liposuction.

If you travel a lot on business or the two of you are separated for long periods of time, its even more important to surprise your lover once in a while. Leave them some goodies like their favorite snack hidden under the pillow before you leave. If they're traveling, hide something in their luggage.

One surefire winner is to give them a Red Hot Survival Kit - A love note, a greeting card (women especially love greeting cards), a small package of Oreo cookies, a picture of you in your Speedo swim trunks, and a miniature bottle of their favorite shampoo.

10. FEATHER A COZY LOVE NEST

Augment the ambience with sensuous smells, candlelight, and romantic music. Make your bedroom an attractive place to be. Stimulate ALL FIVE of your lover's senses. Add some fresh flowers, buy some new sheets. Fluffy goose feather pillows. A new quilt. Textures that want to be touched. Place an aromatic potpourri on the night stand.

Try some candles. (No flashlights, please.) Soft music. If you have one, make a fire in the fireplace. After some wine, lead your lover into the bathroom where you have candles all around the bathtub brimming with bubble bath. Help bathe them, gently caressing their back (or other fun places) with a sponge. Afterwards, tenderly smear their back with lotion.

**CREATE THE MOOD FOR A THUNDERSTORM
AND LIGHTNING WILL EVENTUALLY STRIKE.**

RED HOT REVIEW
"THINGS YOU DO"

1. **TRADING PLACES**
   Doing some of your lover's chores, especially the ones they dread, will give you a fresh perspective on what their life is like.

2. **OPEN UP THE COMPLAINT DEPARTMENT.**
   Ask one another to list "Three Things You Do That Bother Me." Be willing to change behavior that annoys your lover and remember not to get your feelings hurt by the answers

3. **TAKE AN INTEREST IN YOUR LOVER'S INTEREST.**
   It may mean raising tomatoes for you men or becoming a Hulkamaniac for you women but it's time well spent.

4. **GET OUT OF A RUT.**
   Break the monotony of your life patterns and relationship by trying new activities together.

5. **SPEND SOME PRIME TIME TOGETHER.**
   Once a week spend an hour alone with just your lover even if its just taking a walk together. Going to the movies doesn't count.

6. **REACH OUT AND TOUCH THE ONE YOU LOVE.**
   As touch is our primary language, hugs, rubs, and snuggles are very important.

7. **SMILE AT YOUR LOVER.**
   A smile is contagious and a definite mood elevator.

8. **EVERY SO OFTEN DO SOMETHING OUTRAGEOUS.**
   Phony blunders, practical jokes, and other childish behavior are important steps on the road to Red Hot Monogamy.

9. **SPRING A SURPRISE ON YOUR LOVER.**
   Unexpected displays of love and passion always are appreciated.

10. **FEATHER A COZY LOVE NEST.**
    Make your bedroom an attractive place to enjoy one another in by stimulating all five senses. Ambiance always augments desire.

CHAPTER 6

THINGS YOU WRITE

Communicating through the written word is a powerful technique. But there's more to it than just scribbling down a note and handing it to her.

The secret to having the maximum impact is that...

THE MEDIUM IS THE MESSAGE!

It's not just WHAT you write, but HOW you deliver it.

1. <u>THE SECRET MESSAGE</u>

Hide a message in your lover's belongings, somewhere where you know he or she will find it when you're not around. The note can be as straightforward as a simple "I love you" or more provocative.

LADIES, write a naughty saying in his filofax on some future day. Try something like, "Tonight when you get home, after the kids go to sleep, you have an APPOINTMENT WITH ECSTASY." Or leave a note in his wallet, on the lawn mower, in his briefcase or gym bag that says, "Looking forward to seeing you later and especially to the *GLAND* finale tonight." You could fax it to him at work. If you had some red hot sex before he went to work, an appropriate note might be..."I love the way you get *UP* in the morning!"

MEN, you can hide a love note in a cereal box so that it tumbles out when she has breakfast. Hide it in her underwear drawer or slip it into her purse. Or write it on a roll of toilet paper, or with soap on the bathroom mirror.

2. BE A LONGFELLOW

Try some poetry. Although a simple "I love you" is always good, silly little love poems are also very effective. Here are some examples:

ROSES ARE RED
VIOLETS ARE NEAT
CAN'T WAIT TO GET YOU
BETWEEN THE SHEETS

ROSES ARE RED
DAISIES ARE FREE
JUST A KISS FROM YOU
BRINGS ME TO MY KNEES

ROSES ARE RED
VIOLETS ARE SWELL
IF YOU WANT TO COME HOME FOR A NOONER,
I'LL NEVER TELL

Belly flops are okay here. The more outrageous and goofy, the better.

3. BUY PLENTY OF STAMPS

MEN, ladies LOVE to receive greeting cards. And for no special reason or occasion. And a card *mailed* to her office or home seems to have greater impact than just handing it to her in person. Send her a thank you note for a fun evening or for planning that bounce back weekend at the Motel 6.

LADIES, the same for you. Even if you've been married for fifty years, sending your husband an unexpected card will have him beaming.

YOU DON'T NEED ANY PARTICULAR REASON - JUST DO IT!

One of my RED HOT MONOGAMY seminar attendees told me the following story. While dating a young lady, they enjoyed a delightful picnic one beautiful afternoon several years ago.

Late fall. Leaves turning. At sunset, he suggested a walk in the woods. Anyway, later that week he sent her this letter...

"Dear Fellow Nature Lover,

Just a quick note to thank you for the most enjoyable walk through the woods you suggested after our picnic on Saturday. I particularly enjoyed your pointing out Venus and Pluto from the dorsal recumbent position you so thoughtfully suggested. The climax of the evening was when you pointed out Uranus and...Thank you for a delightful tour through the heavenly bodies.

With stars in my eyes,
Professor Eureka Bramblebush"

In the interest of good taste, I edited out the rest of the line about "Uranus". Needless to say, that fall he became quite an expert on astronomy.

4. HOMEMADE HALLMARKS

You can always send your lover a humorous greeting card. But it's more effective if you make your own. Fold some colored construction paper in half. If you don't have any, just fold over a piece of white bond. Use some bright colored pens. Here are some ideas to get you started:

OUTSIDE:	INSIDE:
Did you know that **when men haven't had** **enough sex** **they tend to...**	Squint.

Rub your hand on this word. **HORNY**	Just wanted you to feel horny.

Don't open this card unless you're in the mood for sex.	Doesn't take much, does it?

ATTENTION, EARTH PERSON: I am a creature from Outer Space. I have transformed myself into this card. Right now I am having sex with your fingers. I know you like it because you're smiling. When you're finished, please read me again because...	**I'm Multi-Orgasmic.** **Thank you.**

5. THE STORY CARD

This style of card remains popular, thought you're going to create one specific to your relationship. And the more outrageous, the better.

You can create these around a certain theme, such as that recent weekend you spent together or about the perfect evening you've just shared.

Here's one for you **MEN**. **LADIES**, just change the appropriate words. Tailor it to your lover's humor. You can make it as goofy or as sweet as you desire.

SELECT THE ONE BEST ANSWER THAT APPLIES TO YOU:

I get off work early and pick you up for a drive down the coast. After our romantic dinner at your favorite seaside restaurant, you suggest a stroll along the beach. Leaving my car at McDonald's, we saunter along the frothing surf, avoiding the disgarded medical waste that has washed up on shore.

As we rest to watch the sunset, I pull you close to me and we fall into a tight embrace. Even though the sand is digging into your back, you can't take your eyes off..

1) **my blazing azure orbs.**

2) **the sun suddenly colliding with a super nova.**

3) **the two sperm whales humping just offshore.**

4) **David Hasselhoff stuffing his speedos.**

5) **the lizard that crawled up my shorts.**

In the heat of passion, you rip off my Domino's pizza shirt. I feel your heart, pounding in your chest. You move your face close to mine. Your tongue darts out. We kiss deeply. You reach down towards my throbbing male hardness. I'm so turned on you could tell time with my erection. "Oh yes!" I cry out in ectasy when you stop to inform me that...

1) **my nasal hairs are tickling your moustache.**

2) **that's not mayonnaise.**

3) **my turgid pickle is about to be bitten by a sand crab.**

4) my breath reminds you of a meat packing plant.

5) Surprise! I have one of those too.

6. <u>WESTERN UNIONIZE IT</u>

Send your RED HOT LOVER a Telegram. It really gets their attention. Whenever I get one, I'm hoping that I won the Publishers Clearinghouse Sweepstakes. Send it to them during the day at work. Or if she's a housewife, have it delivered to the beauty shop when you know she'll be there. Again, greater impact. Here are a few ideas for you:

> **YOU HAVE JUST WON THE FAMOUS** (*your name*) **WIFE OF THE CENTURY SWEEPSTAKES [STOP] FIRST PRIZE IS A WEEKEND OF SIN AND DEBAUCHERY IN LAS VEGAS WITH THE SEX MANIAC OF YOUR CHOICE [STOP]**

> **CONGRATULATIONS [STOP] YOU HAVE JUST WON THE COSMO "SEXIEST MAN OF THE YEAR" CONTEST [STOP] FIRST PRIZE IS A ROMANTIC EVENING OF DINNER, DANCING AND ROMANCE WITH THE WOMAN OF YOUR CHOICE BUT WHO MUST BE** (*your height*) **TALL AND ANSWERS TO THE NAME OF** (your name) **[STOP] CALL** (*your number*) **FOR DETAILS [STOP]**

Remember, little acts of creative thoughtfulness can score big points.

7. <u>THE TREASURE HUNT</u>

Instead of just handing a present to your lover, send them on a treasure hunt. Give your RED HOT LOVER a 3 x 5 card with a clue on it. Compose the hint in the form of a poem or couplet. The first card will hint at the location of the next card and so on.

MEN, here's an example:

CARD # 1

> **I'm glad you made it home tonight,**
> **Look for your next clue where you'd find something "LITE"...**

She finally looks in the ice box and taped to the Bud Lite can is the next clue.

CARD # 2

> **You're far from through, but don't be feeling down and blue,**
> **I've got a nice surprise for you. So now take a look in your shoe...**

She's getting a little more excited as she scurries into the bedroom, digs around the piles of shoes every woman has, and finds the next card.

CARD # 3

> **It's always nice to hear you moan when you get the bone,**
> **I think you're honing in on it if you go to the phone...**

By now she'll be in a frenzy of excitement and anticipation. As she dashes from phone to phone, she finally finds a tiny note taped to the mouthpiece of the one upstairs.

CARD # 4

> **I want to give you what I got,**
> **Look for your next clue someplace that gets hot...**

You can make the clues a little tougher as you go - it adds to the suspense. She might look in the fireplace. No luck. She'll contemplate, then rush over to the stove. Nothing. Her eyes will light up. The oven! She throws it open and finds that great, personalized present you bought her.

A variation of this is to take it out of the house. You could send your lover to a phone booth, call with the next clue, then send them to the flower shop to pick up one present and another clue that would lead them to a restaurant where you would be waiting.

8. MAKE YOUR OWN HEADLINES

MEN, get out the old Polaroid again and take a picture of you at your BEST, if you know what I mean. Slip the photo under her pillow or in her purse with a note. Or, if you've got a computer, print out a headline like "Porn Star Arrested" or "Sex Maniac Escapes" and glue it and the picture in an appropriate spot in your daily paper.

LADIES, you can do the same. Take a picture of your face and have a headline that announces "Luckiest Woman In The World."

9. GOING TO EXTREMES - BANNERS AND BILLBOARDS

Many computer printers can produce a banner-like sign. If your partner has just gotten a promotion, print out a six foot long "Congratulations" and hang it over the doorway. Or rent a billboard and put one of your love poems on it. Advertise your love by renting some space on the side of a bus. The ultimate is having a skywriter display your message of love or lust.

10. BE A MICHANGELO

Include drawings and cartoons in things you write are. Not artistic? You don't have to be. Here is one of my favorites.

An ideal place for this is on the bathroom mirror drawn with a bar of soap. You can put any caption you want, but I like just saying "Hi." You can also draw this on a napkin and slip it to her at a party. Others canvases for you to try are a roll of paper towels or roll of toilet paper or that roll of fat on your stomach.

Other "paints" to use are food items. The next time you are having some Cheez Whiz and crackers, draw a heart on a cracker and hand it to your lover. Or maybe you could write your initials and theirs. Serve your lover some cookies on a platter in the shape of a heart.

Other canvasses include the great outdoors. The next time you're on a walk or hike, stop unexpectedly and draw a heart in the dust with you and your lover's initials. If you're at the beach, draw it in the sand. Or tromp out with your feet a ten foot heart in the snow. One farmer in Iowa was known to cut a one acre heart for his girlfriend in a field of hay.

One of my favorite canvasses is the inner thigh and favorite mediums is Cool Whip. Note that either your finger or tongue make an excellent paint brush.

RED HOT REVIEW
"THINGS YOU WRITE"

1. HIDE A SECRET MESSAGE IN YOUR LOVER'S BELONGINGS.
It can be a simple "ILY" or something more naughty. Remember that for all of the "Things You Write," the method of delivery is as important as the message.

2. USE "ROSES ARE RED" STYLE POEMS.
You don't have to be Will Shakespeare to score big points - just try to make the ines rhyme. The more outrageous, the better.

3. RED HOT LOVERS SHOULD SEND THEIR PARTNERS LOTS OF CARDS.
Women especially love to receive cards. Keep Hallmark and your lover happy.

4. HOMEMADE HALLMARKS ARE EVEN BETTER.
Take some construction paper and make your own greeting card.

5. CREATE A MULTIPLE CHOICE STORY CARD FOR YOUR LOVER.
Of course, there is no <u>one</u> correct answer. Tie these in with recent discussions, trips, or events.

6. SEND YOUR LOVER A WESTERN UNION TELEGRAM.
Few things are more exciting than receiving a telegram telling you that you've won some big sweepstakes for being sexy.

7. SEND YOUR LOVER ON A TREASURE HUNT.
Use 3x5 cards with obscure clues to lead your lover on a wild goose chase around the house or the neighborhood till he or she finds their surprise.

8. MAKE YOUR OWN HEADLINES.
Type out a headline, such as "Sex Maniac Escapes" and paste it in your local paper. Add an appropriate Polaroid, then slip it into your morning paper.

9. GOING TO EXTREMES
Written messages can also be placed on billboards or other outrageous places

10. BE A MICHANGELO AND DRAW A PICTURE OF AFFECTION.
Whether it's drawing a heart in the sand at the beach or using Cheese Whiz on the inner thighs, a picture is worth a thousand words, if not more with inflation.

CHAPTER 7

THINGS YOU GIVE

We all like to receive presents. And you would think that giving your lover a present would be rather straightforward. But to really do it well, there are a few things you need to know.

Let's begin by finding out...

WHAT IS A WOMAN'S FAVORITE ROMANTIC GIFT?

A recent study of women - both married and single - revealed the answer to be...

FLOWERS!!!

Different cultures have vastly different ideas of romantic gifts. The women of Northern Siberia are reputed to show their affection toward men by throwing slugs at them.

The old mainstay is a dozen roses. **MEN**, should you send the lady you love some? Maybe. But it is almost too blase' nowadays. A single rose in a bud vase with a tender note can be very effective. Don't know what to put on the card? Ask the florist taking the order. They are often very hip to the correct verbiage. Or think about sending a poem on the card like the ones discussed earlier.

It's best to send them to her at work rather than to her at your house if you live together. Why? Because...

WOMEN LOVE TO SHARE THE EXPERIENCE WITH THEIR GIRLFRIENDS!

They love to brag about their lover or husband, to shout to the world and tell everyone how wonderful you are.

Give flowers sparingly. One woman I know received a magnificent cut flower arrangement every Tuesday like clockwork. After awhile, it lost its effect. Keep them off balance by mixing up all the techniques in this book. I wouldn't send flowers more than once every couple of months. And **LADIES**, for something out of the ordinary, send your man some flowers. Remember in romance, always do the unexpected.

Whether you decided to use flower power or not, you need to know about the...

FIVE RULES OF GIFT GIVING

1. <u>LESS IS MORE.</u>

Again I want to stress that too much wood smothers the fire. You don't want them to think that you're trying to buy them off. **MEN**, unless it's a real special occasion, stay away from those emerald necklaces or diamond earrings.

HOW MUCH SHOULD I SPEND?

The answer is as much as you want. I'm not saying you should never buy your wife those diamond earrings or your hubby that Sears sit-down lawn tractor with the green sun umbrella, but the point is...

A recent survey of women ages 17 to 70 revealed that 4 out of 10 women would much rather hear the words "I love you" than receive a present.

Make a cassette tape of your lover's favorite songs. Give a little "color commentary" between each one: when you first heard each song together, how in love you felt that night. Then sneak the cassette into their car.

MEN, a TEDDY BEAR with a little note that says something like, "this is for those nights I can't be with you" is always nice. You might also make a trip to Victoria's Secret for a pair of sexy underwear.

Send your lover a self portrait of you - or a *part* of you - that you've drawn. If the sketch looks more like fingerpainting than a Michangelo, try a photograph of you or your little buddy. You might want to leave that studded leather jock on and just show off that nice little STIFFIE you're working on.

For these "private parts" I would suggest using a Polaroid unless you want the guys at the sixty minute photo place to be snickering every time you come in.

LADIES, a little cleavage or silk teddy shot is always effective. If you want to go to extremes, there are actually photographers that specialize in professional boudoir portraits - check your local yellow pages.

Don't forget to enclose a suitable caption. You **LADIES** could put something like, "You're the cream in my coffee." **MEN**, try, "You're invited to a private screening of the following COMING ATTRACTION." *(After receiving this, my wife commented that it looked more like a "short subject" to her.)*

Make a COUPON BOOK - take a bunch of small, 3 x 5 cards and staple them together. Use different colors. Draw some borders around them or paste some stars on them. Make them all different. Here are a few ideas on what to include:

This valuable coupon entitles the holder to one FREE "Mongolian Muscle Massage." *(I have no idea what a "Mongolian Muscle Massage" is, but it sounds like fun.)*

"This certificate good for one ROMANTIC DINNER at the restaurant of the holder's choice." *(At the bottom write)* "Void where prohibited. Must be used by *(some future date)*."

"This coupon is good for two free tickets to the romantic movie of your choice."

This coupon entitles the holder to HALF OFF a photo session with Aldolfo (*or Aldolfa*), the XXX Photographer.

This coupon entitles you to a free shampoo and blow dry by (*French variation of your name, i.e., Pate' for Pat*), that famous Beverly Hills hair stylist and former men's room attendant who specializes in trendy "do's" and naughty "don'ts."

Other things for a **WOMAN'S** book would be foot rubs, manicures, doing the dishes, and so on. For **MEN,** offer them a new pair of hiking boots or maybe some golf balls.

2. NOTE THE NOTE

With any gift, the note is very important. Be imaginative. Avoid cliches. Tie the note in with the gift. If you're giving him a pair of Nikes, tell him something like, "I'll always be running after you." Or, "Just Do It...with me!" If you've given him a new coffee machine, write "I hope this perks you up." When you hide that Slo-Poke candy bar in her purse, stick on a note, "Looking forward to giving you another Slo-Poke later!"

3. ACCESSORIZE THE GIFT

Always do a little extra to the gift. Always have it WRAPPED. If it's a coffee cup, give her some gourmet coffee with it. If it's a new jogging suit, buy her a pair of bulky white socks to go with it.

4. PERSONALIZE THE GIFT

Be creative when you buy your lover something. The more personal it is, the better. Something tied into their interests. For her, a book on antique furniture or gardening. Surprise him with theater tickets for his favorite play or maybe with sports tickets for the big game.

If he's a Trekkie, go ahead and pay big bucks for one of those communicators or go for one of William Shatners' old toupees.

Try to tie the gift in with something she has mentioned lately. Maybe she saw an ad on TV for a new perfume. Surprise her with it. Plus it...

SHOWS YOU LISTEN TO HER.

LADIES, if you just can't think of what to get, remember that most men love gadgets, electronic stuff, or tools. "Boy Toys" if you will. Remember that...

REAL MEN NEVER GROW UP, THEIR TOYS JUST GET MORE EXPENSIVE.

MEN, if you're stumped on what to get and you're not too great at handcrafts, remember that most women love stuffed animals.

> *"The gift without the giver is bare. Rings and jewels are not gifts but apologies for gifts. The true gift is a portion of one's self."*
>
> *Sir Lancelot*

5. ACCEPTING THE GIFT

Whatever it is you receive, smile and thank your lover for it. Even if you don't like it or need it. NEVER say things like, "It's too expensive" or "I'd never wear that." **LADIES**, if it's some plaid shorts that went out of style in the 50's, try them on immediately and act excited. If you absolutely do not want it, wait at least 24 hours, then tactfully bring up the subject about exchanging them for a Chanel purse.

Also try to use the gift as soon as possible. **MEN,** if it's a new tie, wear it the next day. **LADIES,** splash on that new cologne the next time you go out. Also important it to know what kinds of things not to give your lover. Here are suggestions for...

TOP TEN GIFTS TO AVOID

1. Jeffrey Dahlmers' *Making the Best of Leftovers* cookbook.

2. Slow motion footage of Baseball players scratching themselves.

3. Muffins made of stuff combed out of ZZ Tops beards

4. Black and Decker Liposuction machine.

5. 32 oz. spray size of Pepperidge Farm Cologne.

6. Copy of *The Amish Joke Book.*

7. Free prostate exam by Meadowlark Lemon.

8. Jock strap from one of Keebler elves.

9. Coffee table size edition of *"The Barney Frank Pop-up Book"*.

10. Sexy Lace outfit once worn by J. Edgar Hoover.

RED HOT REVIEW
"THINGS YOU GIVE"

1. **FLOWERS ARE A WOMAN'S FAVORITE ROMANTIC GIFT.**
   Less is more - one rose can send more of a statement than a dozen.

2. **EXPENSIVE ITEMS AREN'T NECESSARILY BETTER.**
   Save those diamond earrings for a very special occasion and create your own presents. The gift can be inexpensive, but the appreciation will be priceless.

3. **NOTE THE NOTE.**
   Tie the note in with the motif of the gift and avoid cliches.

4. **ACCESSORIZE THE GIFT.**
   Socks with shoes, tie with shirt. Always have them wrapped and always include a card.

5. **PERSONALIZE THE GIFT.**
   Tie in the present with your lover's interests, hobbies, or desires.

6. **ACCEPT THE GIFT GRACEFULLY, EVEN IF YOU DON'T NEED IT OR LIKE IT.**
   Wait till the newess wears off before talking about exchange or returns. And if you are going to keep it, use the gift as soon as possible.

Chapter 8

THINGS YOU DO IN THE BEDROOM

T he MOST IMPORTANT thing for you to remember is...

GREAT SEX STARTS IN THE HEAD, NOT THE BED!

Remember that if you hit the home runs in the kitchen - by the time you get to the bedroom all you have to do is run the bases.

Let's assume you've used the techniques I've given you and you've made your lover feel special. You've given them the security, romance, and conversation they need - you've slugged that home run out of Foreplay Stadium. But the game's not over yet. There are a few fine points you need to know about base running.

EROGENOUS ZONES

To begin with, a major part of this is finding just the right trigger points, that is, those sensitive areas that really turn your lover on. These erogenous zones often change with time, and especially after marriage. Men are often oblivious to these, so I've listed a few for you.

WOMEN'S EROGENOUS ZONES
BEFORE MARRIAGE

1. Buttock   3. Ear   5. Nipples

2. Back of Neck   4. Inner Thigh

WOMEN' S EROGENOUS ZONES AFTER MARRIAGE

1. Anything from Saks Fifth Avenue

2. American Express Card, especially Platinum

3. His and Her walk-in Closets

4. Mercedes 560 Sl Convertible

5. Gallon of Ben and Jerry's Cookie Dough Ice Cream.

Now its time to show your lover what the "Red Hot" really means. You're at that point in space and time between Foreplay and Afterplay, a place where ectasy and pleasure reign surpreme, the RED HOT ZONE. And to gain admittance, there are some physical techniques you need to know.

PRACTICE THE TECHNIQUES IN THIS CHAPTER AND YOU'LL HAVE YOUR LOVER THRASHING AROUND IN BED LIKE A LANDED SALMON!

1. ACME POWER TOOLS

Pick the size, shape, and color you desire. These personal talismans come highly recommended by many women.

MEN, most department stores carry a nice selection of vibrators. I would pass on Hasbro's Slippery Pocket Partner and Popeil's three-in-one vibrator, heat massager and magnifying glass. Pick one that's not too heavy (otherwise your hand gets exhausted). Battery power is also a plus (the cords never are long enough and get snagged on the most embarrassing things). One with a variable speed motor is also nice.

Start out on your lover's feet or back. Take at least thirty minutes. Throw in some soft kisses along the way. Work your way along the inside of her thighs, around the back of her knees. Tease her. Give her a sample and take it away. Go back to her inner thighs. Sprinkle in a few kisses on the back of the neck,

52

ear lobes, palms of her hands, or behind her knees.

These are what I call the KINDLING AREAS. Get the sparks going here and things will heat up very quickly. We're talking hotter than a magnesium flare. MEN, the thing you DON'T want to do is just start grinding away on the "bingo bud."

"Some are born to greatness, some achieve greatness and some have greatness thrust within them."

Hal Lee Luyah

Become a concertmaster and direct a symphony of love. Consider Beethoven's Fifth. Da, Da, Da...**DA**! It starts quietly, but crescendos to a thunderous climax.

Turn up the temperature some more by using both the vibrator and lingual and even manual stimulation on her simultaneously. Use your other hand to caress her breasts. *[NOTE: Do not use it to click the channel on the TV remote control.]* Some women may desire a light touch while others may want you to grind away.

LADIES, you can also use the vibrator on your mate, working out the tension on his back, neck, and thighs. At the appropriate moment, turn control over to him.

2. COOL WHIP ON THE HIPS and RIPPLE POTATO CHIPS

I'm not a big Cool Whip fan unless it's in my coffee. The same goes for ice cubes which I prefer to put in a glass of Diet Coke. But if you're into "Arctic Torture" or "Cream Delights," go for it. Warm oil is also a possiblity.

You might want to feed each other grapes or other erotic foods. One of my favorites is Ripple potato chips. "Big deal," you retort. I forgot to mention that you have to feed them to each other using only your THIGHS!

BELLY SHOOTERS, where you slurp the beverage of your

choice out of your lover's belly button could be an interesting way to quench your thirst. LADIES, thin slices of Kiwi fruit laid in a trail over your lover's body can also be a fun way to get your MDR of Vitamin C and "P".

3. <u>HOT WATER</u>

Take a glass of hot water, set it on the night stand. Let your lover think you're just taking a drink of tap water. Start your love-making. Progress to oral sex. Before part A gets inserted into slot B, break away and take a mouthful of the water. Act like you're just thirsty. As you kiss your partner's private parts, however, let some of the warm water slowly trickle out. *(Note: plan ahead and have a towel handy.)* After that, expect your monthly water bill will skyrocket and your bed may sustain structural damage, but such are the hazards of Red Hot Monogamy.

You can also experiment with different fluids. Other things to try are Pepsodent tooth paste in front of a fan, Creme de Menthe, and Listerine.

MEN, are you married and not having oral sex? Here are a few lines to try.

---

10 WAYS TO PLEAD FOR ORAL SEX

1. I wouldn't lie to you honey, it tastes just like whipped cream.

2. Joe's wife does it for him all the time.

3. Hey, it's even got vitamins in it.

4. You'll get used to it.

5. I promise this time not to come in your mouth.

6. I'll do it for you.

7. Sure, I'll respect you.

9. If those hairs tickle you nose, I'll shave them.

10. What do you mean? I just washed it last week.

---

4. GET OUT THE "CUM" CAM

Set your camcorder on the dresser and leave it on record. Be sure to get your lover's permission.

When I saw what I looked like naked I decided to stick to filming vacations and birthdays. But if it works for you, go for it.

A variation of this is a POLAROID PARTY where you photograph interesting parts of one another's anatomy. For you parents, make sure the kids don't find the photographs later.

5. EROTICA

Try some of those erotic magazines or XXX videos. Some couples can really be stimulated by this. But it has to be a <u>mutual</u> decision.

According to recent studies, more women than men use pornography as a sexual stimulant.

I really love some of the titles such as " Riding Miss Daisy," "City Lickers," "On Golden Blonde," "When Harry Ate Sally," and "Malcom XXX." A seminar attendee of mine followed my suggestion and tried this technique out on his new girlfriend, a demure, kindergarten teacher. At the next class, he noted he had received a rather icy reception. When I queried him what film he rented, he replied, " THE ANALIST, PART II". Use some common sense on selecting the video.

LADIES, if you're shy about this or don't know how your lover will react, you could always pretend that the geek with pimples the size of pepperonies at the local video store gave you the wrong tape and as long as you've got it, you two might as well watch it.

6. LADIES SHOULD ALWAYS COME FIRST

MEN, I'm sure you are all aware of the fact that women take longer to reach orgasm.

Try to let your partner have an orgasm BEFORE you even get close, using whatever method you like, vibrator, manual, or lingual. (For those of you into extremes, I would suggest maybe belt sanders or tire jacks.)

> *The average time for a woman to reach orgasm is eleven minutes. By contrast, our furry friends aren't as lucky. Our close relative, the poor baboon, takes a mere eight seconds and 15 thrusts to complete intercourse. Lions average four seconds - I think that's about where I was in high school.*

Let them beat you to the "gland finale." Lagging a few steps behind is okay. Save yourself and wait for her subsequent orgasms and try to reach that moment of ecstasy together - the reason being that when women have orgasms, the second and third are the most intense. Like a summer thunderstorm approaching in the distance, think of her first orgasm merely as heat lighting before the big storm hits. Remember:

LADIES SHOULD ALWAYS COME FIRST!!!

MEN, after your lover *thinks* she's satisfied, whisper that you can't hold out any longer, it's coming. However, men, I want to you to fib a little. Tell her this when you're, say, only eighty percent of the way there. Moan and groan like it's happening.

The excitement of your expected orgasm often will push your lover to a new level of ecstasy.

MEN, after this great performance, NEVER ask a woman, "Did you come?" It kills the moment. Do the Monday morning quarterbacking later.

The most common time for sex in the US is 11 p.m. on a weekend. Also the New England Journal of Medicine reports that women are, on the whole, 30% more sexually active during a full moon.

For you **LADIES**, you can get things cooking with the following Red Hot Recipe:

SIZZLING SAUSAGE SANTA FE

Step One, *heat up a tube of K -Y Jelly by holding it under hot water.*

Step Two, *squeeze tube and introduce the lubricant into your "love oven."*

Step Three, *have your partner slowly introduce sausage.*

Step Four, *repeat till meat is sizzling.*

MEN, another ploy is to make love while your lover is blindfolded. Using a blindfold deprives her of her visual senses, thereby accentuating touch and sound. It allows tension to build between touches - she won't know where the next sensation will *come* from. (And you can watch a ball game with the sound turned down, and she'll never know.)

7. F-117 FOREPLAY

This form of foreplay is just like the Stealth fighter - you never know its coming till it's too late. It's seduction disguised under good pretenses.

During the day, make a bet you know you're going to lose. Don't be too obvious. The winner gets a BACK RUB. It can be anything you want but this is especially effective. Darn it. You lose. That night have your lover lay in bed. Leave their clothes on. Start at the head and work your way down to their neck.

Massage each of the vertebral bodies. Walk down the thoracic spine. **MEN**, DON'T make a move for the breasts. Make it strictly a PG massage and not X-rated. Try lightly tracing the alphabet on her back. Then do it backwards. Firm pressure. Punctuate it with a gentle kiss on the neck or ears. Move down to the lower back and buttocks. Knead them like two wonderful pieces of dough.

Make a sprint for the goal line and you've fumbled. Score your touchdown later. For now, play it cool. Tease them. Sprinkle some comments like: "Oh, that's better, relax, I feel all that tension going away. Good."

When you're finished, they'll roll over. Give them a gentle kiss on the forehead. Wait for them to respond with a kiss. It's downhill from there but still tease them; act like you're not that interested in making love. Even try telling them you're impotent tonight. They'll try to disprove you everytime.

A variation of this is to put two tennis balls in a tube sock, spaced about two inches apart. Position the balls on either side of your partner's backbone. Gently roll them up and down, allowing the balls to massage her back, neck and shoulders. Experiment with different types of balls.

The feet are one of the most appreciative recipients of touch with over 72,000 nerve endings in each foot. Reflexology can be very erotic.

A GOOD FOOT RUB WILL BRING ANY WOMAN TO HER KNEES.

A LYMPH massage of the face is also very relaxing. With firm pressure and slow, symmetrical movements, rub your lover's forehead, the inside of their eyes, moving down to the other side of their nose and cheeks.

8. DON'T BE CONSISTENT

MEN, vary your pitches. The point is, just don't burn in the fastballs. Throw your lover a curve once in a while. Mix it up.

LADIES, change your usual position, your cologne or perfume, your technique. Keep them off balance, never knowing what or where to expect love-making to happen.

Plan on having sex all over the house. Exotic locations like on the dining room table add a degree of excitement and naughtiness that your partner will love. Do it on the washer during the spin cycle.

The Mangaians of Polynesia are the most highly sexed people in the world, having sex at least three times a night.

Sometime right in the middle of sex, stop and start giving your lover oral sex. **LADIES**, this coitus interruptus followed by *knobus slobus* will have your man melting.

MEN, when the rhythm of your thrusts is quickening, withdraw and slowly reintroduce your penis, just barely inserting the head. Pop it fast and slowly withdraw. Or leave it outside of her and rub it on her. Another favorite is the "pearl necklace" or so-called "Pasedena Necktie,", where you pull out at the last moment and shoot those 200 million spermatozoa on her. Try drawing a cupid heart on her chest.

9. HIGHER AND TO THE LEFT

Don't be afraid to give directions or make requests. "Not so hard. A little lower....Not THAT low."

For instance, some women may like forceful, direct stimulation while others will desire the gentlest touch. Others may like a combination of the two. Some men may get excited when you lightly fondle their testacles during sex, others may want you to juggle them. Or maybe gargle them. The point is, TELL your lover what you like.

10. ASK YOUR LOVER WHAT HE OR SHE LIKES

Don't be embarrassed. **LADIES,** ask you lover, "Is that's

good, honey...what do you want me to do?" Or, "Hon, how about this?"

MEN, don't be too proud or confident. Don't trip over your machoismo ego when it comes to lovemaking.

ASK HER WHAT SHE LIKES!

Some women may volunteer this information while others won't. "How's that, honey? Is it too heavy? How does that feel?" This improves her enjoyment and also shows you care. You may also want to discuss this before you get into the bedroom.

11. <u>KISSING MAYONNAISE, JELL-O, AND TIMBER WOLVES</u>

Women love to be kissed. They love passionate, deep, tight, eyes shut kisses on the lips. Keep a little firmness in those lips so that she doesn't think she's kissing a bowl of Jell-O.

Mix in some tender, butterfly kisses on his or her closed eyelids or inner thighs. The back of the neck is also a very strong trigger area, relating back to some kind of basic animal instinct. Timber wolves do this a lot. Try a gentle, biting type kiss here and watch your lover howl.

Vary your kissing technique. Keep your lips firm sometimes, soft others. Try folding your lips over your teeth and bite your lover's tongue. Don't overdo French kissing. Soft and slow and moist but not gooey. Nobody likes to feel like they're kissing a bowl of Mayonnaise. Do some nose rubbing.

By the way, the Samoans prefer to smell each other rather than kiss.

Move your hands up and down your lover's back while you kiss them. Touch their face while you're kissing them. Gently rub your finger over their lips. Slowly place your finger in your lover's mouth. Break off every now and then and stare longingly into their eyes. Then return to the kiss. Take a mouthful of wine and pass it back and forth.

Tongue superiority isn't something you always want to have. Don't be an iguana, zapping your tongue in and out with metronome regularity.

12. "OH MY GOD!"

Are you chatty or do you just make a few moans with an occasional ecstatic invocation of the deity thrown in?

Ask your lover what she likes. Some lovers may be perfectly satisfied with an inarticulate grunt. Some lean more towards terse bulletins from the front (or wherever). And others require a more complex exchange with a real narrative thrust.

> *"Mrs. Robinson, do you think we could say a few words to each other... this time?"*
>
> **Dustin Hoffman in *The Graduate***

People equate absence of noise with absence of passion. Inspired pillow talk is good but don't go for phony histrionics or rantings.

THE ABSOLUTE WORST THING YOU CAN SAY *IN FLAGRANTE* IS YOUR FORMER LOVER'S NAME.

Avoid overdoing it, doing a play by play, or blow by blow. No lover wants a horizontal Howard Cosell.

Whisper in your lover's ear, "You're really sexy" or "You really turn me on." It's also better if you don't "Groan Alone." Tell your mate that you appreciate feedback too.

When your partner is basking in the afterglow, just don't roll over on your stomach and start snoring. Hold them, tickle them. Caress their body - and their ego. Tell them how much you enjoyed making love.

You don't always have to be clever or have a snappy repartee. A simple "It couldn't get much better than that" or "You're the best lover in the world" will suffice nicely.

13. MUSIC DURING SEX

Music was the highest rated aphrodisiac in a study by the Institute for Advanced Study of Human Sexuality in San Francisco. Stick to instrumental music. "The Best of Slim Whitman" could be a little distracting. A CD of romantic piano music is always a nice mood-setter.

14. THE ULTIMATE IN GENITAL STIMULATION

Anthropologists have found men throughout the world go to extreme lengths to improve their sexual equipment. Men in Borneo insert brass wire, bamboo and ivory into the end of their penis as added vaginal stimulus. In nearby Sumatra, the Batak tribe slice open their penis and insert pieces of stone which become embedded when the wound closes over. We're talking major stimulation of the G-spot.

MEN, I'm not suggesting that you men start collecting rocks but the point is well taken - do what it takes to please your lover.

WOMEN, ask your lover what he likes. As I mentioned above, some men like to have their testicles tickled while having sex. The point is...

LEAVE NO STONE UNTURNED IN YOUR QUEST TO PLEASE YOUR LOVER.

Recently doctors have started doing fat injections into the penis to increase its size. Silastic rods can also be put in the shaft to give you a continuous erection. However, we all pale in size to the African bull elephant who's penis weighs about seventy five pounds. Among mammals, however, Mr. Big is the blue whale with a penis averaging over ten feet in length!

MEN, sometime in your life you may not be able to get it up. Don't panic. Things like this happen to the best of us. Below I've listed some of the reasons for this.

REASONS FOR MALE IMPOTENCE

1. Her moustache tickles.

2. She asks, "Is it in yet?"

3. Afraid your wife might come home early.

4. That darn Salmon smell.

5. She calls you "Bubba" by mistake when having orgasm.

15. PHEROMONE HURRICANE

Stimulate all of your lover's senses. Odor is a potent aphrodisiac for both men and women. First of all...

GOOD HYGIENE IS A MUST.

Some say, however, that bathing washes away our natural pheromones. Thus, we now use artificial scents as a replacement. It's interesting, however, that many of our favorite perfumes and colognes are actually made from animal pheromones.

Musk from male deer in Asia is so strong that it cannot be washed off polished steel. Civet is another common ingredient that comes from the anal glands of the civet cat of Africa. I don't think you want to know what Ambergris is, but let me just say it's what happens to be found in three hundred pound, waxy lumps in the intestines of sperm whales.

Too much cologne or perfume can be a turn off. Suggest more than overwhelm. **MEN,** I would recommend *not* perfuming your pocket rocket. Better to stick with that lingering scent of "Irish Spring" rather than to overpower them with Aramis. **LADIES,** bath oils can give your entire body a refreshing, aromatic presence.

16. PREVENT THE PREGNANCY BUT PRESERVE THE MOMENT

Two points need to be made here. First, plan ahead. Have whatever supplies you need at hand's reach. I know it's a headache. That it takes away from the spontaneity dealing with diaphragms, stuffing those sponges, or wrestling with rubbers. It could be worse. In some parts of Africa the most popular contraceptive device is a pessary made of elephant and crocodile dung.

In Medieval times, Dutch caps were invented and the most practical was the half lemon that was put over the end of the penis during sex with oral sex indulged in afterwards. Perhaps, that's why Mona Lisa's mouth is twisted into that smirk.

Secondly, rather than try to brush over it, make it part of the sexual act. That way you don't lose the momentum. **MEN**, rather than struggle, trying to nonchalantly slip on that condom with one hand, ask your lover to help you with it. Tell her that she's got you so turned on, you don't know whether or not it's going to fit.

LADIES, don't be embarrassed and run into the privacy of the restroom to pop in that spermicide suppository or diaphragm. Ask HIM to do it while you continue kissing and touching one another. Foreplay is Team play.

17. WHAT REALLY TURNS ON A MAN

LADIES, a recent study of American male sexuality revealed the following proportions of men who found these stimuli most exciting:

WHAT REALLY TURNS A MAN ON

1. A woman taking the initiative

2. Perfume

3. Lacy lingerie

4. A women using sexually explicit language while making love

5. Vaginal odor

6. *Taking off pants and sitting on nude picture of Anne Nicole Smith.*

LADIES, taking the initiative with men can also pertain to situations outside the bedroom. Unexpectedly unzipping his pants and giving him oral sex in the car on the way home will always put a smile on your lover's face.

RED HOT WARNING!

MEN, IF YOUR LOVER IS NOT INTO GARTER BELTS AND LACY LITTLE THINGS, APPROACH THE SUBJECT GENTLY. YOUR FIRST LINGERIE PRESENT SHOULD NOT BE A PEEK-A-BOO, VELCRO PAIR OF LEOPARD SKIN PANTIES WITH BUILT-IN VIBRATOR AND BUTT PLUG.

Just as important for you **LADIES** to know is what NOT to do.

WHAT REALLY TURNS A MAN OFF

1. Heavy make-up

2. Leg or underarm hair

3. Heavy Menstruation

4. Poor personal hygiene

5. Third trimester Pregnancy

6. *Watching Hidden Video of Turkish Prison Shower Room*

18. KAREZZA

Karezza is a technique described in Hindu sexual treaties whereby men remained with erect penises inside their partners for hours on end. There are accounts in Chinese literature of busy Mandarins attending to their jobs, signing documents and discussing urgent matters with visitors while maintaining an erection in their concubine.

MEN...Do you realize what this means for the American male? Just think of it, watching Monday Night Football, eating a pizza, AND bonking all at the same time. Seriously, the point is to make lovemaking last as long as you wish. Don't be in a hurry. Practice Karezza till either parts of your body start going numb or you break the bed.

19. AFTERPLAY

Afterplay is just as important as foreplay, and is often neglected as time goes on, usually about a week after you take your honeymoon.

AFTERPLAY BEFORE MARRIAGE

1. SHE gets up and gets HIM a washcloth.

2. HE gives HER back rubs and tickles till she falls asleep.

3. HE washs himself off in the shower before going to sleep.

4. In the middle of the night, HE rolls over to HER and whispers "I love you."

5. They BOTH avoid the wet spot in the bed.

AFTERPLAY AFTER MARRIAGE

1. HE makes HER get up to turn off the TV.

2. HE rolls over on his stomach, farts, and immediately starts snoring.

3. HE decides to wash off in morning.

4. In the middle of the night, SHE rolls over to HIM and shouts. "Give me my half of the blanket you bed hog!"

5. They BOTH avoid the wet spot in the bed.

Afterplay is the decompression, the release, the sharing of the act of lovemaking. Gentle rubbing, and stroking, both physically and verbally, are part of the afterplay package. Whisper tender terms of endearment. Tell your lover they're the greatest - the best lover in the world. Do this whether or not it's true.

Use a warm washcloth and cleanse your lover. If you have enought energy, take a shower or bath together. In short...

REAFFIRM YOUR LOVE.

20. <u>THE SECRET OF THE WORLD'S GREATEST ORAL SEX</u>

Ask a man what his greatest B.J. of all time is, and without a doubt he'll single out one or two women that were the best. The problem is, LADIES, if it's not you, he may be reluctant to tell you. Or he may just lie to you and tell you that you're the best - which is what I would recommend he do.

But **LADIES**, why shouldn't YOU be the BEST? You all have the same two hands and mouth anyone else does. All you need is a little practice. And some time spent eating slimy, raw oysters won't hurt either.

First, ATTITUDE counts for a lot. By that I mean a man wants to feel like YOU'RE really into it - that you not just doing it because he want's you to. Be enthusiastic, grunt and groan. Some of you may be naturals in this regard. Others, whether it be from upbringing or genetics, are more reluctant. If you value you're relationship, give it your best. You *can* learn to enjoy it.

Second, get him hot by kissing everywhere down there BUT on the old Schwanz.

Third, there are certains parts of a penis that are more sensitive and certain techniques to use on them. Since this varies from man to man, it's best to ask your lover what he likes. Remember that practice makes perfect. For postgraduate training, I would suggest you ladies rent a Traci Lords video.

MEN, lest we forget, women also enjoy oral sex. What I said for the ladies also applies to you. Ask them what they like, work on your technique, and get used to eating at sushi bars.

RED HOT REVIEW
"Things You Do In The Bedroom"

1. **ACME POWER TOWELS**
   Vibrate your partner to new heights of ectasy.

2. **THINK UP NEW WAYS TO EAT COOL WHIP, POTATO CHIPS, AND KIWI.**

3. **EXPERIMENT WITH ORAL SEX HELPERS.**
   Get yourself in Hot Water and have a Pepsodent smile.

4. **BE THE STAR OF YOUR OWN X-RATED VIDEO.**

5. **EROTICA.**
   Porn films can be very arousing. But be sure to check with our partner first.

6. **LADIES SHOULD ALWAYS COME FIRST.**
   This is the secret for giving a womam multiple orgasms.

7. **F-117 FOREPLAY.**
   Stealthy seduction. Start with a back or foot rub. Take it slow before you go low and don't let on to your real intention.

8. **DON'T BE CONSISTENT.**
   Vary the location and the technique. Keep it fresh and exciting.

9. **TELL YOU LOVER WHAT FEELS GOOD.**
   Communicate your desires.

10. **ASK YOUR LOVER WHAT THEY LIKE.**
    Don't assume they like what you do.

(cont.)

"Things You Do In The Bedroom"
(continued)

11. **LEARN HOW TO KISS LIKE A TIMBER WOLF.**
    Bite the back of the neck. Women espcially loved to be kissed. Keep a little firmness in those lips and avoid too much tongue (mayonaise mouth).

12. **"OH MY GOD'S!"**
    Give positive feedback during sex, even if it's only a groan.

13. **ROMANTIC MUSIC IS A GREAT APHRODISIAC.**

14. **THE ULTIMATE IN GENITAL STIMULATION**
    Do what it takes to please your lover.

15. **PHEROMONE HURRICANE**
    Stimulate all of your lover's senses including smell.

16. **BIRTH CONTROL DOESN'T HAVE TO DESTROY THE MOMENT.**
    Plan ahead. And do try to disguise the act of contraception - incorporate it into the act.

17. **WHAT REALLY TURNS A MAN ON**
    The top three are women taking the initiative, perfume, and sexy lingerie.

18. **KAREZZA -**
    You don't have to be a Hindu to practive COITUS CONTINUUM INFINATUM

19. **REMEMBER THAT AFTERPLAY IS JUST AS IMPORTANT AS FOREPLAY.**
    Reaffirm your love after the act of lovemaking.

20. **THE SECRET OF THE WORLD'S GREATEST ORAL SEX.**
    You too can be the best. And only your lover can tell you how. Remember that attitude is just as important as technique.

CHAPTER 9

THE 21 MINEFIELDS OF MONOGAMY

Just as important as what you DO, is what you DON'T DO.

> *"What you leave out of a great CASSEROLE is just as important as what you put in."*
>
> **Dr. Hannibal Lecter**

Watch out for and avoid these tripwires and booby traps at all costs. The beneficial effects of all your good deeds can be wiped out in a milli - second. Dash through the Minefields of Monogamy and your relationship will last as long as a Columbian judge

Some of you MEN may already be stepping on these MINEFIELDS and not knowing it. WHY? Because many women choose to suffer silently, kepting their emotions tied up inside.

Most men can externalize their feelings, i.e., yelling, screaming, and hitting inaminate objects during a temper tantrum. A flash like when you ignite the lighter fluid on the charcol. Women are more like the red hot ambers that smolder for hours or days. The only thing you may notice is a detached attitude or some reticence. She may bury her head in a book or spend more time sewing or on the computer.

This can be a dangerous situation. In the interest of the well being of us MEN, I've listed below a few broad hints that your wife may not be too happy with you...

TOP 10 WARNING SIGNS FOR MEN THAT YOUR RELATIONSHIP MAY BE IN TROUBLE:

1. You find Gopher Go Away nuggets in chocolate chip cookies.

2. She buys you steel bristled Q-tips.

3. New easy chair she bought at the San Quentin garage sale has leather restraints and is plugged into the 220.

4. Stun gun falls out of negligee pocket.

5. She uses Chinese finger torture for diaphragm.

6. Offers to trim your toenails with Electric Hedge Trimmer.

7. Buys Dr. Kirvorkian's First Aid Kit for you.

8. Mixes Super Glue in with your Preparation H.

9. Installs new seat belts in your car made of razor wire.

10. Fixes dinner using scraps from meat plant dumpster.

So if those large candles on your birthday cake look suspiciously like dynamite, you may have a problem. Before you blow, take responsibility for saving it. Remember...*MEA CULPA*.

1. DON'T BE A SCROOGE

It's okay to be frugal, but don't be cheap. If you can afford it, go first class whether it's out to dinner or on a trip to Hawaii. On special occasions, treat your partner to a romantic dinner at place where the dinner salads cost more than a Casio watch.

Be good to your lover and yourself. You both deserve the best once in a while.

LADIES, when buying him say, a tie, don't always head for the clearance rack with last year's styles. Buy him a Polo knit rather than that K-Mart special.

MEN, if you're going to buy her something, buy the best you can afford. Don't buy the imitation Giorgio scent at the local discount drug store - pop for the real thing.

MEN, don't use your pocket calculator to figure out to the penny what fifteen percent is on your dinner tab. If you've got it, give a good waitress a twenty percent tip.

Also, MEN, if you are going for a big ticket item, like diamond earrings, don't get a couple of splinters.

Women have a sixth sense about this. They can spot a nickel and dime guy and it's a big, with a capital "B," turnoff. Here are a few guidelines women use...

A WOMAN CAN TELL A MAN IS CHEAP WHEN HE:

1. Switches from Coke to Vess Cola.
2. Uses slugs in condom machine.
3. Waters down the Perrier.
4. Uses Knackwurst casing as birth control device.
5. For Birthday present, buys you Milli Vanilli album.
6. Recycles aluminum foil from Preparation H suppositories.
7. Uses Jack in the Box napkins for toilet paper.
8. Only flushes toilet once a week to save water.
9. Favorite dish is Road Kill Stew.
10. Uses balloon taped to dash as passenger air bag.

2. DON'T STING YOUR LOVER WITH HIDDEN BARBS

This back door method of criticism is another big "no-no." Avoid couching sarcasm in a request. Don't conceal an insult in a question.

MEN, say you just came home from an exhausting day at work and you're starved. While you're patiently waiting for dinner, your lover or wife is casually chatting away on the phone over a lot of nonsense to one of her girlfriends. She waves hello and proceeds to blabber on for another fifteen minutes. You're getting hotter than the meatloaf. That's it. You leap off the sofa and stride over to her.

Don't sarcastically mutter, "When you're not so BUSY, I would like to have dinner." Minus one thousand points for you. You're a big boy now - take care of yourself. Snack on an apple. Or better yet, nibble on her neck, saying, "I'm sooo hungry I may have to eat you for dinner."

Hidden barbs can also be called BOOMERANG BARBS - these snide remarks invariably come back to haunt you at some distant time in the future.

LADIES...Say he's working at his desk at home when you tell him dinner's ready. He yells back, "Be there in just a second." The minutes tick by. You call him again. And again he tells you he'll be right there. You're hotter than the shrimp scampi you slaved over. How can he be so inconsiderate?

Instead of unloading on him, making a scene, and throwing away dinner, just start eating without him. Give him his space and his options. You could try bringing dinner to him. Or go back into his office and rub his back - tell him not to work so hard. Don't nag him to the dinner table. Try telling him the sooner he gets done with dinner, the sooner he gets his special dessert. "What special dessert?" he asks. I'll leave that up to you.

3. DON'T BE LAZY

Pull your share of the load. **MEN**...for couples that live together, if you both work, don't expert HER to do all the house work, the laundry, and iron your shirts. If she's occupied with other things, pitch in and help. If the sink is filled with dirty dishes that have been there so long they're growing Microbe X, don't nag at her to do them - YOU wash them.

LADIES, if he is kind enough to do all this for you, recognize and acknowledge it. If not, resentment will smolder, sometimes for years. Five years from now during some argument, he will remind you about the time he did the dishes when you had the flu.

LADIES, if that man of your dreams parked his tush in front of the TV all night long, ask him for a little help. Just don't take it upon yourself. However, you must do it in the right way. You don't want him to become defensive and lapse into that same old speech about "how hard he works."

Taken to the next level, don't be lazy in pursuing your life's dreams. Women especially admire ambition in a man. Don't just sit around watching your life pass you by. Jump in there and make something happen.

4. DON'T KEEP THINGS TO YOURSELF

If things bother you, let you lover know rather than let things gnaw inside of you. Every so often open the "complaint department" for one another.

MUSHROOMS, LIKE PROBLEMS, GROW IN THE DARK.

Take an inventory of each other's annoying habits. You may think its insignificant, but it may be a really big deal to your lover.

LADIES, maybe your man forgets to put the toilet seat down. In the cosmology of the universe it's no biggie but it drives you crazy. Or, the fact that he never hangs up his clothes. Don't let the resentment build up inside you. But don't nag him about it either.

WARNING! DON'T HIT YOUR LOVER OVER THE HEAD WITH A LAUNDRY LIST OF COMPLAINTS.

Only pick out a couple of things that bother you the most and GENTLY bring them to their attention. And be sure to ask them if YOU are or are not doing something that annoys them.

AT LEAST ONCE A MONTH ASK YOUR PARTNER IF THERE'S ANYTHING YOU DO THAT BOTHERS THEM.

5. DON'T BE A SLOB OR SLOBETTE

Okay, **MEN**. Be honest. Can you fit in a pair of Meatloaf's pants? Take a look at yourself. If you were your wife, would you want to make love to you? Is gravy your beverage of choice?

Do you come home and sprawl on the sofa, slurp a beer, your belly jiggling as you belch, stuff down zillions of M&M's, and then moan, "Honey, is the pizza here yet?" Does your stomach expand at the same rate as the Milky Way?

LADIES, are you so heavy that you burn out the escalators in the mall? Do your stretch marks show up on satellite recon photos? Do you only put an inch of water in the bathtub when you get in so that it doesn't overflow? If so, it may be time for you to hit the gym and practice a little GIRTH CONTROL.

MEN, after work, when you change into your casual clothes, don't be too casual. You probably think that since you're married or living together, you don't have to worry about that stuff, that you can be yourself. WRONG!

Your lover will glance at that old sweatshirt with the holes in it and your wrinkled shorts and think to herself that you don't care. It's not fair but it's the way women think and so do men. It's okay to be a slob once in a while, but once in a while make an effort to look especially good, even if it's just another evening at home. She'll feel that you dress up for total strangers at your job but don't care enough to look nice for her. Whatever you wear, always practice good hygiene.

The same applies to you **LADIES**. Take a few moments to freshen up. Feather your moppage. Throw on some lip gloss. Wax off that moustache. It only takes a few seconds.

Remember how you looked and acted when you were courting? Don't take your appearance for granted. Make yourself more appealing to your lover. **MEN**, get a haircut, wear that new sports jacket. **LADIES**, get a facial, get your nails done, wear those new spiked heels you've been saving. And both of you, if you're not already, should start working out more.

> *If exercise could be put in a pill, it would be the most widely prescribed medicine in the world.*

6. DON'T BE BORING

Take a look in the mirror. Are you that much fun to be with? **MEN**, is your big hobby racing slot cars? Or sitting on the front porch counting cricket chirps?

Read the newspaper. Read a book. Any book. Keep yourself informed. Have a hobby. In short...

MAKE YOURSELF MORE INTERESTING!

If you don't want a boring relationship, YOU CAN'T BE BORING! **LADIES**, fill those dinners together with discussions of world events. Read him a joke book. Go out with another couple. An interesting couple. A group of fun friends can add energy to a relationship.

Discuss your future projects and entrepreneurial ventures. During dinner, try some mental exercises, like trying to invent something. Play "My Fave Five" game (your favorite five movies, songs, vacations, etc.).

Gossip about people you know. Plan how you're going to corner the real estate market or get rich in the ant farm business.

7. DON'T WIN ARGUMENTS

Knock down, drag'em out scream fests - what good are they? Have you ever really had an argument with someone you love that has solved something? Think where you're going to be when it's over. Will things really be any different? Will the issue be resolved?

ARGUMENTS ARE A WASTE OF LOVE

> *"If it weren't for marriage, men and women would have to fight with strangers."*
>
> *Unknown*

If you lock horns with your lover, I just want you to know that the playing field isn't level. You can never WIN. I know this doesn't seem fair, but it's the way it is. It's okay to have spirited discussions and frank disagreements. But screaming, threatening, ranting, or raving is strictly *verboten*. So is one of the females favorite manuvers...pouting. Communicate!

LEARN HOW TO LOSE ARGUMENTS - AND SAVE YOUR RELATIONSHIP.

I don't expect you to be a jellyfish. Nobody likes a "yes" person. Have your opinion. State it. Discuss it. But gently. Try to see the situation through the other person's eyes. Give you lover's point of view a chance. Try saying "MAYBE" instead of "NO!" "PERHAPS" in place of "FORGET IT!" Go along to get along.

> *"My wife gives good headache."*
>
> *Rodney Dangerfield*

ARGUMENTS ARE LIKE QUICKSAND, THE MORE THE STRUGGLE, THE DEEPER YOU SINK.

8. DON'T LOSE YOUR TEMPER

For whatever reason, losing your temper ranks right up there next to arguments in tearing apart relationships. Sure, we're all human. There will be times when the Mount Pinatuba of anger will erupt. I've been there. Ready to blow. Like the time my wife wouldn't sell me Park Place when I owned Boardwalk.

INSTEAD OF SEEING RED, TRY SEEING PINK.

Once you get the hang of it, more subtle hues will follow. Don't lob H-bombs at the one you love because the fallout will linger for months. At all cost, avoid any kind of physical violence. It's an instant way to nuke your relationship.

9. DON'T BE A "HEY VERN" TYPE

People like a lover who is intelligent, who can speak well and is knowledgeable about the world. We're not talking particle physics Ph.D., but the ability to conjugate verbs would be nice.

You can always try dropping a few of the following POWER WORDS on her. They're fun to use at those stuffy cocktail parties.

Egregious. Assiduous. Insouciance. Adulate. Hubris. Truculence. And don't forget *vis-a-vis, tete-a-tete,* and *quid pro quo.*

I'll admit that sometimes I'll say "impasse" and the silent "e" will skip out and get pronounced. "Respite will rhyme with "despite." I'll rhyme Yeats with Keats. Proust with Faust. And suddenly the mask will be ripped from my face and everyone will know that I'm really Jethro Clampett in disguise.

Be more than a ho-hum hominid. Pick one new word a week. Use it in your conversation with the one you love. You can also make up some of your own and really drive people crazy at cocktail parties like: *farfalesence, yutiginous, or cohumerate.*

Of course, you could always borrow those fake glasses Kevin Costner wears to appear more intelligent.

For some of you, it may be diffcult to tell if your mate is as smart as he claims. For this reason, LADIES, I'm giving you the...

TOP 10 WAYS TO TELL IF YOUR LOVER'S NOT AS SMART AS HE CLAIMS:

1. Wonders how those refs on World Federation Wrestling can miss so many illegal holds.

2. Wants to reserve place in Mount Rushmore for Shemp - *when we all know it should be Curly.*

3. Thinks he could solve world enery crisis by harnessing static cling in John Madden's pants.

4. Tries to start "the wave" while watching World Series on TV.

5. Wonders why the drinking fountains are so low in the public restrooms.

6. Thinks Robert Goulet is behind this whole Bigfoot thing.

7. Give's finger to Mr. Gotti's limo after it changes lanes without signaling.

8. Can't figure out why Klingon empire doesn't join UN.

9. Always relieved when Tweety gets away from Sylvestor.

10. Buys Sports Illustrated for free "Best Of NFL" video - ***not*** for the swimsuit issue.

---

10. <u>DON'T ALWAYS BE THE CENTER OF ATTRACTION</u>

MEN, are you an "I," "Me," and "Mine" kind of guy? Does

the world revolve around you? Do you always have to be the center of attraction and attention?

LADIES, do you always get to pick the movie? Are YOUR problems always the biggest? Is whatever you do or think the most important thing?

IF YOU WANT YOUR RELATIONSHIP TO GROW, DON'T MAKE YOUR LOVER LIVE IN YOUR SHADE.

If things are going bad, it's okay to cry on your lover's shoulder. Don't be a limp wimp. We all have bad days, but don't throw her a PITY PARTY every night. Wouldn't it destroy the image if Superman went around whining about his hemorrhoids bothering him?

Make YOUR LOVER the center of the conversation. Don't constantly talk about yourself and what you did today. Share the spotlight. Take an interest in them and their life, their job, their hobbies, their health. Let them know you care about what they think. Ask their opinion and give them an equal voice.

11. DON'T POSITION YOURSELF AGAINST YOUR LOVER'S PASSIONS

LADIES, don't force him to choose between you and golf or tennis or fishing! MEN, the same for you and gardening, bridge, or shopping for clothes.

The answer is, if you can't beat them, join them. Read a little about his or her hobby so you can join in or at least have an intelligent conversation with them about it.

12. DON'T THROW ROCKS

Married people sometimes begin to think that they have a right to criticize their partner or to make those helpful suggestions. It seems that men have a greater tendency to do this than women, maybe because they like to fix things.

As we discussed above, there will always be things your partner does that annoy you. Don't concentrate on who she's *not* but who she *is*. Overlook that rock in your shoe. Live with it.

ACCENTUATE THE POSITIVE AND IGNORE THE NEGATIVE.

What do you do if the rock feels more like a boulder?

TOSS A PEBBLE!

Another facet of this problem is that what you THINK is a pebble could be a boulder to the other person. **MEN,** say that as you're walking out the door to a dinner party with your wife or lover, you make the off-hand comment, "looks like that dress is getting a little tight." You really didn't mean anything by it, but most women will be CRUSHED by such a comment, probably putting them in a bad mood for the rest of the evening. The female ego is a fragile thing. Women are wired different that men.

BE AWARE OF THE DIFFERENCES AND BE CAREFUL WHAT YOU SAY.

Okay. So you've got a rock in you shoe. I don't want you limping around the rest of your life. There will be some things that grate on you so much that you have to let her know about them. And that's okay. But pick the right time and place. **MEN**, don't clobber her with it when she's in the middle of fixing dinner for those ten people you're having over that night.

STEP ON YOUR LOVER'S FEET EVERY DAY, AND PRETTY SOON THEY WON'T EVER WANT TO DANCE.

The same applies to you **LADIES**. Both of you should LIMIT this type of criticism to no more than twice a month. That way you and your lover will feel safe that you can be yourselves. Nothing is more destructive to one's ego or to a relationship than the feeling that your partner is constantly watching you, judging you, or critiquing every little thing you do.

NEVER LAUNCH VERBAL TORPEDOES

More than just a barb, a prick, or a sting, these heavy duty personal insults will come back to haunt you for years. **MEN**, always remember - THEY NEVER FORGET!!!

Avoid expressions like "How can you be so stupid?" or "Bill says his wife wants to have sex all the time." Make a snappy comment like, "the varicose veins on the back of your legs look like an AAA map of the midtown freeway system," and you will demolish your lover's ego and sink your relationship with one shot.

NEVER compare your lover's physical attributes or lack of them to other people. **LADIES**, if you're at the beach, don't tell him he should go on a diet while you stare at a tan, twenty-year-old lifeguard with the chiseled ab muscles.

MEN, if she has small breasts and is sensitive about them, avoid any jokes about eraser tips or cupcakes. Don't comment that that blond babe at the next booth has a cleavage deeper than the Mariana Trench.

When you love somebody, these off-hand remarks become etched in their mind. And never make remarks about her anatomy or funny odors, even if they're made in jest. A comment like this will hang around in her memory longer than the hole in the ozone.

And both of you should NEVER THREATEN DIVORCE. It's the deadliest of them all. Guaranteed to destroy your lover, your love life...and the relationship.

13. <u>DON'T GLORIFY PREVIOUS LOVERS</u>

"ALL OLD LOVERS ARE DIRT." Please repeat this phrase ten times to yourself. At all costs, avoid discussing past romances, old flames and former main squeezes. NEVER tell your lover everything about a past romance. If pressed, reveal only the barest of details.

Am I saying not to tell them the truth? *You bet.* It's in the past. Fine. What difference does it make? Your husband or wife will always compare themselves to your past lovers, even if it were twenty years ago. Guaranteed.

LADIES, if the name of a former stud of yours should come up and your lover starts to run him down, agree with him. Immediately state with supreme conviction, "I was so stupid. I don't know what I ever saw in him." Or try something like, "I forgot all about him. Comparing him to you is like comparing a Piper Cub to the Concorde. You take me higher, faster, and further than I've ever been."

The same applies for you **MEN**. If the lady of your life starts asking you about a former tryst of yours, immediately start degrading her. "Oh honey. I forgot completely about her. I must have been an idiot to go out with her - she was so gross even farm animals wouldn't let her pet them."

14. DON'T GET YOUR SHORTS IN A KNOT OVER THE LITTLE STUFF

Do you have quirks or habits that aggravate your lover? Things that push their hot button? **LADIES**, does the man of your dreams drink out of the milk carton? Or forget to put the toilet seat down?

YOU GO INTO A MARRIAGE WITH YOUR EYES WIDE OPEN. TO STAY MARRIED KEEP THEM HALF CLOSED.

(Most of the time I have to really squint.)

Work on minimizing your traits or habits that bother your lover. Try to overlook your lover's faults - consider them quirks. Be tolerant. Balance a fine line between being overly sensitive and overly tolerant, between being a DART and a DARTBOARD.

Try not to be a Perfectionist. **LADIES**, does your man just toss his socks haphazardly into the drawer while you have them rolled and sorted according to color?

However, you women do have a problem...more of a fault if you could call it that. You you fall in love, you tend to be VERY TOLERANT of us men. But, there are certain points where you should draw the line. To help you define this line, I've included a few guidelines for you to know...

TEN WAYS TO TELL IF THIS MAN ISN'T FOR YOU

1. Is saving his money so he can get matching tatoo on other side of forehead.

2. Big ambition is to be that guy in Goofy outfit at Disneyland.

3. Doesn't unwrap hemorroid suppositories before chewing.

4. Can't figure out why they don't just get some bum to Squeegee off that smeared lens on the Hubble telescope.

5. Collects and trades your tampons with poker buddies.

6. Does air guitar to Slim Whitman.

7. Tries to pick up other girls at pool by dandling turkey neck out of swimming trunks.

8. Has oozing, infected gash from crushing beer cans against his forehead.

9. Picks up hitchiker wearing necklace of human ears.

10. Puts finger in butt; makes cork-popping sound.

MEN, does your wife have the ability to see microscopic collections of dirt particles while you don't notice them till they're large enough to support commercial agriculture? Does she insist on buying that Calamari flavored yougurt?

You might think couples would **not** pick mates with opposing habits. Such is not always the case. The answer again is TOLERANCE. Be a little less perfect.

TRY TO MEET YOUR LOVER HALFWAY.

If you feel YOU MUST say something, do it from the 'I' perspecitve rather than the "YOU." This means you should never begin your sentences with "YOU."

LADIES, you might be tempted to utter,"**YOU** never put the toilet seat down!" Using "YOU" is a form of psychological finger pointing. Rather, begin your sentences with "I." "**I** don't like having to always put the toilet seat down."

ALWAYS BEGIN COMPLAINTS WITH "I" RATHER THAN "YOU".

15. DON'T BE AN ADOLPH

Nobody likes a dictator. **MEN**, don't order her to have the house clean when you get home.

Avoid expressions like, "You'd be nothing without me," "My way or the highway," or "Kiss my Ring."

MEN, we in particular have a problem. We tend to be fixers.

STOP JUDGING AND STOP CORRECTING.

Don't lecture her. She doesn't need it. Don't try to be her father or mentor. You're her lover.

LADIES, don't issue ultimatums. Never *order* him to be home by a certain time or else. Holding a mental cudgel over your lover's head will only make them resent you. Don't try to make them your puppet. Offer your lovemate the chance to INPUT, EDIT, and COLLATE important decisions. Remember, when your karma runs over her dogma, it's time to quit.

One of the biggest "no-no's" is to demand sex. **LADIES,** if your guy falls asleep during the back rub you're giving him and your hormones are peaking, you may have to settle on "self" rather than "full" service. **MEN,** if she dozes off after a long day and you've got a big "stiffy" and are ready for a cavalry charge, blow revelry on your own bugle.

START DICTATING SEX AND YOU'LL SEE PASSION TAKE A HIKE!

Even if this happens several times in a row, live with it. Remember again that...

TOLERATION IS THE SIGN OF A GREAT RELATIONSHIP.

Don't be a scorekeeper. Put your lover's wishes and desires first. That's what being in love is really all about.

DON'T NAG!

Even if you're right. ESPECIALLY if you're right. **LADIES,** nagging will drive a man into a non-communicative state quicker than a 1088 Audit with the IRS.

"Marriage is like a besieged fortress. Everyone outside wants to get in, and everyone inside wants to get out."

Quitard

---

16. <u>DON'T BE "MR. or MRS. RIGHT"</u>

He's a cousin of the Perfectionist. "Mr. or Mrs. Right" is the person who may not always be right, but is never wrong.

Do you stutter when you start to say, "I...I....I'M SORRY"? Do you break out into a cold sweat, your brow furrow, and your lips contort into a sneer when you try to utter "It was my fault"?

When's the last time you told your lover, "Hey, I was wrong. Totally out of line," or "I'm sorry I lost my temper"? Live your life accepting on a daily basis the fact that..."I ERR, THEREFORE I AM." Don't be afraid to say the magic words...

"I'M SORRY."

This is part of life. It's part of the bigger picture of accepting yourself. Then eventually liking yourself.

IT'S ALWAYS EASIER TO LOVE SOMEBODY WHO ADMITS THEIR MISTAKES.

17. DON'T BE AN "N.B.C." (NEGATIVE BLAMER COMPLAINER)

These are the people who think the glass is half empty instead of half full. That every bump in the road is a crevice. The "IF ONLY" type that always laments his present situation, blaming it on something else. *"If only* I had a better job." *"If only* I wasn't so fat." *"If only* my breasts were bigger." *"If only* my boss wasn't such a jerk." *"If only* I was smarter." *"If only* I was rich."

CARPE DIEM..."Seize the day."

Better yet, seize the moment. Enjoy what you've got at hand. There is no past, no future, only the present. With this in mind, don't come home every day complaining and blaming everything that went wrong on everybody else. YOU can set the mood for the whole family. Don't make them tiptoe around on eggshells because you're crabby.

LIVE IN THE MOMENT - IT'S ALL ANY OF US HAVE!

18. DON'T BE A PERRY MASON

All of us want to feel needed and missed. But FATAL ATTRACTION and jealousy only serves to undermine a relationship, slowly eroding the trust between you. An insecure man or woman is very unattractive to their partner.

It's okay to question your lover on what they did or who they met but don't be a drill sergeant. Never accuse them of lying. Keep up the Perry Mason tactics and YOUR insecurity - not another person - may drive your lover astray.

> *"If you get a good wife, you become happy.*
> *If you get a bad one, you become a philosopher."*
>
> **Socrates**

19. DON'T BE WISHY-WASHY

MEN, women like men to be DECISIVE. How many times has your lover asked you, "What movie do you want to see tonight?" and you reply, "I don't care." Or she asks where you want to eat and you tell her, "It's up to you, honey." It's okay to be easygoing, but don't force *her* to make all the decisions. TELL HER that you WANT to take her to Bistro Gardens. TELL HER that you'd LIKE to buy her that yellow linen sports jacket.

Same for you **LADIES**. Give your man some feedback. Let him know *what* restaurant you want to have dinner at and *what* movie you want to see. Don't demand, suggest, but let your wishes be known.

20. DON'T TRY TO CREATE ARTIFICIAL INTIMACY

Don't try to create intimacy by asking probing questions of your mate. Men in particular dread this. Women often do this more than men. These type of discussions will often make your lover feel "crowded."

Conversations alone - intense, analytical discussions that dissect a relationship - are *not* the key to closeness. Intimacy grows out of all aspects of a relationship, especially activities you two share together. And the "activities" don't have to be romantic to promote closeness. Visiting an art museum, shopping for food, seeing a movie - in general sharing life together. And the more spontaneous and unplanned, the better.

21. <u>DON'T CROWD YOUR LOVER</u>

Maintaining the proper amount of SPACE between you is the secret to keeping your RELATIONSHIP together. This can be both physically and emotionally.

"My husband said he needed more space, so I locked him outside."

Roseanne Arnold

I'm also a big believer in separate bathrooms or sometimes separate beds. When you share everything, all the time, there's no more surprises.

Recognize your lover's SEPARATE SPACE. Let them have their own life. As we touched on earlier, let them have their own hobbies, friends, even their own room in the house where they can be alone if they choose. This makes the relationship richer, stronger, more interesting as they bring back new life experiences to share with you.

PAIR BONDING = CREATING A MUTUAL ENERGY MATRIX

Many chemical substances, such as crystals, maintain their shape because of the structural interdependence of the molecules that compose them. The Bucky Geodesic Dome is another example of this - how multiple linking parts can form a structure much stronger than any of its components.

Friends can do this for you. They can inject energy into your relationship.

FRIENDS ARE IMPORTANT - SOCIALLY WITHDRAWN COUPLES WITHOUT FRIENDS ARE THREE TIMES AS LIKELY TO DIVORCE

Do things with other couples. Have barbecues, play cards, go to movies, go on hikes, go cow tipping. Have a barter party where guests bring items they no longer want and trade them for something they do. The same principle can be applied to clothes swapping, book swapping, or junk swapping. *(No wife swapping, please.)*

One of our favorites is called the GROSS GIFT GIVEAWAY. Have your friends wrap up and bring the worst gift they've ever received. Put the gifts in a pile and draw numbers to see who gets what. Say the first person gets an eight-track tape of "Kate Smith Sings - The Best of the Eastern Block Nations' National Anthems."

Then the second person has the option to claim the record or choose another gift and so on until all the gifts are gone. Develop a whole group of friends. They can enrich your life just as your lover does. And help keep you together.

THE BIGGEST BOOBY TRAP OF ALL

It's hard but I'll bypass the obvious pun. There is one Anti-Personel Mine that is the deadliest of all. It's one that we have no control over; that anathema of civilization and modern marriage called...

STRESS

IT'S A KILLER. Not only of your sex life and your relationship, but of your health.

STRESS = THE DEADLIEST DESTROYER OF RELATIONSHIPS

It's hard to be romantic when your roof is leaking, you just got laid off, and your mom is dying of cancer. You may not feel like being a Red Hot Lover for even a minute a day. That's okay. When life sneaks up behind you and whacks you in the head with a baseball bat, who would?

First of all, if you find yourself in this situation, don't hesitate to get professional help from a pyschiatrist or psychologist. They can help you get up on one knee. Then the other.

You can also lean on your lover for support. Don't keep all the hurt inside. Share the grief and disappointment with others who are close to you. Touch them. Hug them. Often times we underestimate how hurt we really are. Stress can manifest itself in many ways. Let your lover embrace you both physically and emotionally.

Exercise and a good night's sleep are excellent stress busters. What about tranquilizers and antidepressants? Except in extreme cases, I'd say no. I'm not for giving patients a thorazine lobotomy or turning them into pharmacological zombies. I'd rather see you heal yourself with your lover's support. Most of all, it just takes ...TIME.

<u>RED HOT REVIEW</u>
"The 21 Minefields of Monogamy"

1. DON'T BE A SCROOGE
It's okay to be frugal but don't be cheap.

2. DON'T STING YOUR LOVER WITH HIDDEN BARBS.
Snide remarks and backhanded insults always come back to haunt you.

3. DON'T BE LAZY.
Do your share of the housework.

4. DON'T KEEP THINGS TO YOURSELF
Open up the complaint department at least once an month but don't go overboard. Limit criticism to one or two things.

5. DON'T BE A SLOB OR SLOBETTE.
Lose ten pounds if you need to. Make an effort to be attractive to your partner. It shows you care.

6. DON'T BE BORING.
Make yourself more interesting. Read the newspaper or a good book. Start a new hobby. Conquer the universe on your day off.

7. DON'T WIN ARGUMENTS.
Because then there will be a loser - not only your mate but the relationship. Arguments are a waste of time.

8. DON'T LOSE YOUR TEMPER.
Instead of seeing red, try pink. A caustic, vitriolic outburst can destroy a relationship in seconds.

(cont.)

9. DON'T BE A "HEY VERN" TYPE.

Spruce up your vocabulary and conjugate your verbs correctly.

10. DON'T ALWAYS BE THE CENTER OF ATTRACTION.

Your lover can't grow in your shade. Share the spotlight. he world should revolve around the relationship, not just you.

11. DON'T COMPETE WITH YOUR LOVER'S PASSIONS.

If you can't beat them, join them. If it means learning about gardening for you men and fishing for you ladies, do it.

12. DON'T THROW ROCKS.

Step on your lover's ego everyday with criticism and pretty soon they won't want to dance at all. If you feel the need to throw a rock, try a pebble instead.

13. DON'T GLORIFY PREVIOUS LOVERS.

Remember that all old lovers are the scum of the earth and you'll do fine.

14. DON'T GET UPSET OVER THE LITTLE STUFF

And remember it's ALL little stuff. Overlook your lover's annoying quirks. But, there's a fine point between being a dart and a dart board.

15. DON'T BE AN ADOLPH.

Don't be a dictator. Avoid ultimatums. And don't nag.

(cont.)

"The 21 Minefields of Monogamy"
(continued)

16. DON'T BE MR. OR MRS. RIGHT.
Don't be afraid to say, "I'm sorry." It's always easier to love somebody who admits their mistakes.

17. DON'T BE A NEGATIVE, BLAMER, COMPLAINER.
Avoid the "if only" phrase. Enjoy what you have at hand.

18. DON'T BE A PERRY MASON.
Nobody likes to get the third degree. Trust your lover.

19. DON'T BE WISHY-WASHY.

Be decisive. Give your lover some feedback. Let them know what you want but without being overbearing.

20. DON'T TRY TO CREATE ARTIFICIAL INTIMACY.
Don't use probing questions to get closer to your lover.

21. DON'T CROWD YOUR LOVER.
Give them their own space, both emotionally and physically. Your lover won't grow in your shade.

STRESS IS THE DEADLIEST OF ALL-
IT CAN DESTROY YOUR RELATIONSHIP
AND YOUR HEALTH.

PART III

CHAPTER 10

A DAY IN THE LIFE OF A SIXTY SECOND, RED HOT LOVER

Now we're going to see just how to apply the techniques and principles presented in this book in a practical, everyday situation. We're going to see how using RED HOT MONOGAMY will change the life of *Henry J. Everyman.*

THE DAY BEFORE

12:34 a.m.

Our story begins with Henry J. Everyman at his office, sleeves rolled up, punching in numbers on his adding machine as he stutters into the phone, "I...I...I'm sure we could work something out, Mr. Barrett. I...ah...I really would like to continue to have you as a client." The other line buzzes; he puts Barrett on hold. It's his wife, Betty. "Hi honey, how's it going? I -" Henry cuts her off in mid-sentence. "Why do you always pick the worse time to call?! I'm busy!" Henry punches off her extension but also disconnects Mr. Barrett. He clinches his fist in anger.

5:46 P.M.

Henry returns home from another frustrating day at the office. He manuvers his Buick Skylark into the driveway and screeches to a halt as his wife's station wagon is parked right in the middle of the driveway. He thinks he can slip by on the right...SCREECH! He rips off the chrome trim on the driver's side of his company car.

Cussing and screaming, he slams his car door shut. He spins and marches to the front door. He tries to spin the doorknob. It's locked! He reaches for his keys and discovers he has locked them in his car! His face narrows into a tight grimace. He jabs the doorbell. No response. He rings it again. Nothing. He shouts for his wife. Knocks on the window. Pounds on the door. After what seems like an eternity, she answers the door, babbling away on the portable phone.

Wife Betty asks, "Honey, why didn't you use your key?" Henry storms past her, "You idiot!" Betty face sags; her eyes moisten as she tells her friend she will call her later.

Betty follows Henry into the bedroom where he's slipping into a paint stained, Grateful Dead T-shirt and holey sweat pants. Henry reads her the riot act about parking in the middle of the driveway - this isn't the first time it's happened.

Betty tries to explain that she needed the room to unload the groceries without banging the car door on the side of the house. She reminds him that he insisted she do that after she dinged the car door unloading groceries. Henry continues with his laudry list of complaints, scolding her for talking on the phone so much.

Dinner is served late again. Henry is already filled from munching on Fritos. During dinner, he only speaks to Betty to ask her to pass the mashed potatoes as he buries his head in the paper.

Betty tells him that she bought him a present. Henry's face brightens. She hands him a copy of RED HOT MONOGAMY. Henry's face dims. He briefly flips through the pages, asking her, "what's this for?" Betty tells him that it looks like it might have some really good ideas in it. Henry snaps into a defensive stance. "There's nothing wrong with our relationship!"

After dinner Henry saunters into the den and parks his frame on his easy chair. He incessantly clicks through the TV channels as Betty sits on the sofa nearby. He is imperious to her choices of channels. She gets up and returns with a stack of papers, balancing the checkbook and paying bills. She comments how she hates doing this every month. Henry responds with, "We all have to do things we don't like to. Everyday I go into that office and work my buns off. Do you think I like it?"

Betty's face shows a trace of hurt, but Henry doesn't notice as he clicks onto the Monday night game. Betty mentions that the neighbors want them to house sit their new puppy, BARNEY. "Would that be okay?" she asks. Henry grunts "yeah" as he starts munching on a bag of nacho chips. Betty goes on about she'd like to have a dog someday, maybe a golden lab or a bloodhound. Henry's only response is a fart that rumbles on the vinyl surface of his easy chair.

Bored by the game and overpowered by the smell, she retreats to the other side of the room and reads *Glamour* magazine. Seeing an article about families, Betty asking Henry about starting a family. Henry responds that they'll talk about it at half-time.

The evening passes. Henry's snoring, passed out on the sofa. Betty wakes him up, brushes the nacho crumbs off his chest. She tells him that eating all that junk food is bad for him. He shrugs off her concern and waddles into the bedroom where he bellyflops onto his side of the bed. Betty finishes brushing her hair and slips into her side of the bed. She, picks up a *Cosmopolitan.* She tells Henry good night. He mutters a reply and rolls over on his side. He's snoring loudly within a matter of seconds. Cut to...

Henry's stomach grumbles. His eyes squint as they try to focus on the alarm clock. It's 1:16 a.m. Too many nacho chips. Belching, burping and farting, Henry heads for the restroom. After finishing, he stumbles into the kitchen and has some cereal to quiet his stomach. He looks around for something to read.

He digs the evening paper out of the trash, glances at it for a moment, then sails it back into the trash can. He picks up Betty's *Glamour,* glances at it for a second, then tosses it back down.

He spots the copy of RED HOT MONOGAMY...flips through some of the pages...he smiles...thumbs a few more pages back...he grins, then laughs. His eyes narrow as he starts reading from the beginning. Cut to...

The clock reads 4:12 a.m. Henry slips back into bed. He's still smiling.

VOICE OVER: A LA "ROD SERLING"

A day in the life of Henry J. Everyman, an ordinary man in a nondescript Midwestern town. A man who last night finished reading <u>Red Hot Monogamy</u>. He's asleep now. The time is 6:47 a.m. When the alarm clocks rings, little does he know his life is about to be changed forever as he wakes up in "The Red Hot Zone."

6:48 a.m.

Henry's eyes blink open to the annoying ring of the alarm clock. He glances over at the night stand where the copy of RED HOT MONOGAMY is. He flips to a few dog-eared pages. A grin creases his mouth.

Wife Betty rolls out of the sack and heads for the kitchen. Henry calls to her, "Betty!" She replies, "I know, I know, I overslept. I'll get your breakfast." Henry replies, **"No, honey, I just wanted to say good morning."** Hiding the book behind his back, he crosses to her and **gives her a smile and a big hug.** Betty shoots back a "what got into you look" and continues on into the kitchen.

4 SECONDS

100

7:15 a.m.

The usual at the breakfast table. Henry flips through the paper as he gulps down his food. Betty gazes out the window. Henry is nearly out of the kitchen when he pauses, a light bulb going off in his head. He turns and **thanks Betty for the delicious breakfast.**

When she tells him it was only an English muffin, **he replies that nobody can butter one like she can.** She beams back a big smile then catches herself, replying, "Henry, what's going on?"

3 SECONDS

7:25 a.m.

As Henry combs his hair in the mirror, he remembers something..."mirror...message...yeah, the medium is the message!" He **writes a love poem on the mirror with soap.** "Roses are red, Violets are blue, you'd look sexier, with my weenie in you." No, he takes a towel and erases it. He can't make up anything he's satisfied with so **he draws a heart with her initials in it**. He feels stupid but does it anyway.

6 SECONDS

7:28 a.m.

Henry checks his Casio - late again. He grabs his briefcase and dashes out the front door.

10:24 a.m.

Another day in the coal mine. Henry can't believe it's almost noon and he's got nothing done. Right in the middle of a meeting with the Big Kahuna, Henry's trying to explain why he just lost a big account.

Just then the phone rings. Mrs. Betty Everyman has placed an emergency call. He grabs the phone, expecting the worse. "Honey," she says timidly, "how are you? I just wanted to thank

101

you for the nice valentine on the mirror and see if you want meatloaf for dinner?" He digs his fingernails into his forehead.

He thinks to himself, "*Gezsus, you interrupted me in the middle of a meeting with the boss for this nonsense?!?" I just lost my biggest client and you're worried about funky buttloving meatloaf!!*" But he remembers about not losing your temper and also about "Things You Say."

Henry does a quick SILENT SCREAM, then politely thanks her for calling and explains how it's not a good time to talk. He whispers that he's looking forward to eating a lot more than meatloaf tonight and gives her a freebie "I love You" to end the conversation. He turns to face his boss who surprisingly, shoots him a smile. "If you treat your clients as nice as you treat you're wife, I think you're going to get that account back in no time."

5 SECONDS

1:12 p.m.

As Henry chews on a soggy submarine sandwich at a lunch counter, he retrieves his copy of RED HOT MONOGAMY out of his pocket and reviews the summaries at the end of each chapter.

While walking back to his office, something catches his eye in the gift shop of the lobby of his office building. **He swings in for a quick purchase. As the sales lady starts to put it in a bag, he asks if she could wrap it. He also picks up a greeting card.**

11 SECONDS

6:14 p.m.

Henry nudges his Buick into the driveway, having fought his way through 55 minutes of gridlock. He's happy to see that Betty didn't park her car in the middle of the driveway again.

6:17 p.m.

As Henry takes determined strides towards the front door, a huge Saint Bernard charges out the door, jumps up and starts licking him in the face, slobbering over his shirt. Betty follows the dog outside. "What the hell is this dog doing here!" Betty replies that she told Henry about the babying sitting the puppy for a few days last night. Henry screams, "This is a puppy!?! I never said that was okay." Betty insists he did.

Henry remembers its easier to love somebody who admits their mistakes. He summons the power for a timid upturn of the corners of the mouth. He tries a little harder, squeezes out a smile and stammers out, **"Ah...A...You're right. I'm sorry, I guess I forgot."** He clears his throat, **"I also want to apologize for blowing my top yesterday. It was bad day and..."** Betty looks like she's ready to cry as she gives him a hug. He hasn't seen her act like this in years.

4 SECONDS

6:35 p.m.

Henry takes off his three piece Sears and Roebuck suit and starts to slip into his favorite pair of baggy, torn Penn State sweat pants. BUT, he remembers about **"looking your best" and instead slips into a comfortable pair of blue Jaymar San-Sa-Belt pants and Madras shirt instead. He even splashes on a little aftershave.**

5 SECONDS

6:41 p.m.

Henry saunters into the kitchen, thinking to himself that with all this Red Hot Monogamy stuff he's doing for Betty, pretty soon she'll build a shrine to him. To his surprise, she all but ignores him and his stylish threads as she blabs on the phone to one of her bridge partners.

He remembers that people and relationships don't change overnight - relighting the fires of passion takes time.

Starved, Henry's ready to dive into his favorite dinner - Betty's meatloaf. His jaw slackens when he spots a package of frozen hamburger on the counter. *"Looks like dinner is going to be late again,"* he thinks to himself. He's so hungry he's chewing his lower lip. *"God dammit! Why can't she have dinner ready when I come home. She had all day long to talk on the phone!"* **Henry is about to let go a boomerang barb like, "Do you think we'll be able to eat sometime this century?" but he bites his tongue.**

3 SECONDS

Henry remembers that your lover's quirks should be ignored when possible. If this really bothers him, he remembers that they should have an air-out session with one another and discuss things that annoy them. But for now, *"go along to get along,"* Henry says to himself as he goes to the frig and grabs a cold one and some chips.

The dog jumps up next to him and starts licking him on the face. Henry starts to giggle as he feeds the dog some chips. He remembers to let the child come out and starts playing with the puppy.

Henry thinks to himself, *"I'm not quite sure what to think about this Red Hot Monogamy stuff. So far the first day has been only lukewarm. But at least it's better than it was yesterday."*

6:54 p.m.

Henry goes to the frig and grabs another Bud. He pops one open and it fizzes all over the sofa. He takes a sip. It burns. He goes into the bathroom and looks in the mirror. He 's got a red spot on the end of his tongue. Looks like a canker sore.

7:08 p.m.

Betty notices Henry munching on the chips with Barney begging for handouts. She hangs up the phone. She tells the pair not to wreck their dinner by snacking. She pops open the oven and takes out a lobster dinner she bought from Henry's favorite seafood restaurant, telling Henry she thought they'd have meatloaf some other night.

Henry's face lights up as he thinks to himself that there may be more to this Red Hot Monogamy stuff than he realized. And he feels lucky that he didn't launch those verbal torpedos at her.

7:18 p.m.

Henry is in heaven. The lobster is great. He blabs on and on about HIS day, HIS boss, HIS clients, HIS problems. **As he munches on a claw, he remembers not to always be the center of the universe. He asks Betty how her day was.**

<u>2 SECONDS</u>

7: 20 p.m.

Surprised at the querry, she goes on and on about her bridge club. **Henry remembers about taking an interest in your lovers hobbies and asks her a few questions about the game and volunteers to learn how to play.** Betty is smiling, bubbly, enthusiastic. Henry realizes that this is the most they've talked in months. And the T.V. isn't even on.

Henry remembers her present. He runs out to his car, then rushes back in with the small box wrapped in pink foil with a card taped to it. She reads the card first, thanking him for it, then tears the wrapping off the small box. Inside is a small stuffed animal...a yellow labrador. She's starts crying.

<u>5 SECONDS</u>

8:24 p.m.

Betty hands Henry the clicker. Instead of watching TV, Henry remembers the part about doing something together and getting outside. **He suggests they take a walk**, just a short one around the block with Barney.

<u>3 SECONDS</u>

8:37 p.m.

Henry and Betty continue their conversation. **He remembers how important touching is and puts his arm around her.** She snuggles closer to him as Barney stops to take a poop.

<u>**2 SECONDS**</u>

8:44 p.m.

They pause at a vista of the city. **Henry starts to tell her how much he loves her but feels funny - he hasn't told her in years. He remembers that being a Red Hot Lover means being vulnerable but he just can't do it.** *Maybe tomorrow,* he thinks to himself. As they saunter down the street, she apologizes for calling him during a meeting today. **He reminds her that she can call him anytime she wants because...SHE IS THE MOST IMPORTANT THING IN HIS LIFE.** *(Homerun, Henry)*

He also remembers about doing things that your lover hates to do and volunteers to work on the checkbook when they get home.

<u>**5 SECONDS**</u>

11:13 p.m.

Henry flosses his choppers and crawls between the sheets. He feels a big fart coming on. Instead of letting it fly, he gets back up and goes into the bathroom.

When he returns to bed, Betty is reading as usual. **Instead of plopping on his stomach, Henry remembers to lean over and give her a kiss good night, but decides to give her a hug instead - at least until the canker sore clears up.**

<u>**2 SECONDS**</u>

Henry tells her that if she wants to trade in her stuffed one for a real puppy, it's okay with him. Betty can't believe her ears. She gives him a kiss on the cheek. Henry's eyes flutter shut.

11:48 p.m.

Betty finishes reading and flicks off the light. Henry is in his alpha wave state of dreaming when he feels something under the covers. It's wet...it's moving...it's a pair of lips on his stomach, headed south. He's about to experience the explosive results of his practicing Red Hot Monogamy's ALL DAY FOREPLAY!

12:56 a.m.

Henry exhales loudly. He's exhausted. Twice in one hour. And with his wife! It's unbelievable! Henry remembers that afterplay is important too but he's so tired. He cuddles with her. As they fall asleep, a big smile spreads across his face. Betty is smiling too. They're on their way to becoming a Red Hot Couple.

TOTAL: 60 SECONDS

VOICE OVER: A LA "ROD SERLING"

Witness one Mr. Henry J. Everyman who found that romance is a state of mind, an attitude...that it's not so much WHAT you do as HOW you do it. Now we see a tired but happy man whose life has been changed forever. A man who spent just sixty seconds today making his wife feel appreciated and adored. A man who now is on that winding road of ecstasy through what we call...The Red Hot Zone.

CHAPTER 11

What is a Red Hot Lover?

Now you know the techniques and methods. You can use these as a guideline and you will hopefully expand on these and add some of your own. In the last chapter you saw how to apply these in a daily situation. You are now, in fact, ready to become a certified RED HOT LOVER. Just what is a RED HOT LOVER?

In a word, I think what makes a Red Hot Lover is *attitude*. But there's a little more to it than that.

***RED HOT LOVERS* HAVE ESP;**
they are tuned in to their partner's wants and desires. Stop on your way home from the office and pick up some Dove Bars for your lover. This ESP gets greater as the relationship grows longer and stronger.

***RED HOT LOVERS* LAUGH A LOT,**
both at themselves and with their lovers. A sense of humor is a prerequisite to Red Hot Monogamy.

***RED HOT LOVERS* ARE SPONTANEOUS,**
able to do things on the spur of the moment, such as taking an afternoon off from work and having an impromtu picnic.

***RED HOT LOVERS* LOVE LIFE,**
and are passionate about it. Red Hot Lovers seize the day, go for

the moment. They enjoy every day and savor every minute with a zest for life and the pleasure of being. They delight in everything they have at hand.

RED HOT LOVERS DON'T WORRY
about what they don't have and they're not even overly concerned about time. They don't dwell in the past or worry about the future. They don't hold grudges. They enjoy life and can adopt that carefree, breezy attitude perfected by postal service workers. They also don't worry about trying to do everything in this book everyday. A Red Hot Lover knows that a little affection goes a long way.

RED HOT LOVERS SHOW THEIR EMOTIONS
and don't resist them. They give them space and then move on, not letting bad moods dominate their life. They know happiness is a habit. They have fun at what they do.

RED HOT LOVERS WORK AT BEING ROMANTIC,
but they also *play* at it. They plan ahead and pull romantic masterpieces, stock up on greeting cards, and always are on the lookout for new ways to make their partner feel special. And find fun in seeing the happiness on their partner's face when they do it.

RED HOT LOVERS DO THINGS FOR THEIR PARTNER WITHOUT BEING ASKED,
such as an un-asked for kind gesture. They know that the surprise and personal gift is most cherished.

RED HOT LOVERS KNOW THAT THEY HAVE TO TAKE THE FIRST STEP,
and when they take the initiative, they give their partner the encouragement for responding in kind. They know that you must give first in order to receive.

RED HOT LOVERS KNOW THAT ROMANTIC GESTURES HAVE NO ULTERIOR MOTIVES;
that their only purpose is to express love and appreciation of their partner.

RED HOT LOVERS NOTICE GIFTS FOR THEIR LOVERS WHENEVER THEY'RE OUT SHOPPING;
they have a part of their brain that's always thinking about romantic ideas. They always put their partner's happiness first and rarely can buy a gift for themselves without getting something for their lover.

RED HOT LOVERS ARE CHEERLEADERS,
being the biggest fans of their partners. They applaud them, encourage them, and provide enthusiasm for them. They compliment and thank their lovers constantly.

RED HOT LOVER'S ULTIMATE GOAL IS TO BE ONE RED HOT COUPLE,
a relationship where the sum is greater than each of the parts. *Team Amore*. Helping one another, working together toward your goals, in short TEAMWORK.

Consider the Anheuser-Busch's Clydesdales. These magnificent animals each can pull 10,000 pounds of weight. Put another one in harness with the first and together they can pull 17,000 pounds. Work on getting the two to work together in harmony and they can pull 25,000 pounds! Just think how much Bud you two can pull.

RED HOT LOVERS MAKE THEIR PARTNER THEIR TOP PRIORITY,
jobs, careers, money, and fame are secondary. A Red Hot Lover knows that their lover is the most special thing in their life and they let him or her know it by words, actions, and deeds.

RED HOT LOVERS ARE NOT MARTYRS;

they don't put their partners first by ignoring their own needs. They put the relationship first. Self-sacrifice always backfires because it builds resentment in the giver. Red Hot Lovers do things because THEY WANT TO, not because they feel they have to.

RED HOT LOVERS KNOW THAT HAPPINESS IS A HABIT;

they have learned to be happy.

Try being totally positive, accepting, supportive, and non-judgemental for seven days. No nagging, negative comments, or barbs. It may just change you're life.

RED HOT LOVERS REALIZE THAT MELTING THE POLAR ICE CAPS OF A FROZEN RELATIONSHIP TAKES TIME;

they treat the stagnated relationship with TINCTURE OF TIME. They give the medicine time to work. They don't get discouraged. Remember what Henry J. Everyman said, that the first day is always the hardest. It takes time, persistence, patience. Just smiling at your partner is a good first step.

For most relationships, just doing the powerful techniques I've given you in this book will have an "effecto immediatoe." However, after twenty years in the deep freeze, don't expect a volcanic eruption of passion. Don't just do ONE NICE THING and expect him or her to fall all over you in appreciation. Remember that a piece of ice thaws slowly, from the outside in.

RED HOT LOVERS KNOW HOW TO LET GO

and be vulnerable. They're not afraid to show their true feelings and to say, "I love you."

It may be hard for some of you Red Hot Lovers to let go at first. Especially you strong silent types. You're going to feel silly, stupid. Vulnerable. You're sure your lover will laugh at you if you try some of these outrageous stunts and goofy things. I hope they do. Laughter is a great first step. Plus laughter burns calories. According to William Fry, M.D., a professor at Stanford University, one hundred laughs a day provide a cardiovascular workout equivalent to ten minutes of rowing.

RED HOT LOVERS *DO* BELIEVE IN TINKERBELL;

they can reclaim the child inside them. They are playful, curious, compassionate, and spontaneous. Red Hot Lovers know how to get in touch with the child inside them and let them free.

And you can too. Most of us have spent our whole life covering up and concealing our defects, shortcomings, and weaknesses. And we're often too reluctant to reveal our whole self to anyone. The child inside may be buried pretty deep in some of you, long forgotten, but he's still hiding in there, waiting for you to let him out. Let him come out and play with the little girl that's inside the woman you love, and vice versa. A man who does this is a real turn-on to women because he possesses many of the traits women adore.

RED HOT LOVERS HAVE THE POWER TO CHANGE

and are flexible. They adapt and overcome.

Changing yourself is hard. Changing other people is even harder - I would rank it somewhere between putting a man on the moon and getting Sonny Bono elected President. Some of you won't be able to change very much. Like anything, "wanting to" is 90% of the battle. But becoming a Red Hot Lover is just the first step. Throughout your whole life you'll continue to be a "Work In Progress." Changing, adapting, improving to different stimuli and situations.

RED HOT LOVERS TAKE RESPONSIBILTY

for making the relationship work. They know it takes two to make it and and one to break it. They also know that they may have some faults and quirks. All Red Hot Lovers know that no matter who's to blame, they have the power to bring the relationship back to life.

I often hear, "It's all <u>her</u> fault that things aren't like they used to be!" In some relationships, everything that goes wrong is "her" fault. Temporarily coating yourself in Teflon has advantages when you come up against something that threatens to sear your soul.

If you lost your job due to cutbacks or the recession, it's okay to be nice to yourself. Deflect the blame and protect your ego from being depressed and disheartened.

Far too many men and women are mired in dead relationships and just shrug and repeat the mantra of the It's Not Me generation, "It's not my fault." Don't let that protective shield of denial destroy your chances for happiness. Put the microscope on yourself for a change.

Finally, I'm going to leave you with a daily checklist. Don't try to remember each and every example and technique in this book. You'll come up with many of your own in no time at all.

What I do want you all to remember is this daily checklist. It's the core curriculum for Red Hot Monogamy.

RED HOT MONOGAMY DAILY CHECKLIST:

1. Did I leave with a hug and greet my lover with a smile?

2. Did I notice something they did today?

3. Was I tolerant of any disappointments?

4. Was I rude, demanding or inconsiderate and if so, did I apologize?

5. Did I make them feel special either with words, actions, or deeds?

As I said before, I can't promise ALL of you RED HOT MONOGAMY. But even lukewarm is preferable to frozen. I do GUARANTEE you that if you follow my suggestions in this book, and spend just sixty seconds a day applying them, your relationship while maybe not perfect, WILL be a whole lot better than it was.

The point is, if you can accomplish that much in a minute, think what you can do in an HOUR A DAY!!!! Well, that's it. Good luck, and feel free to blame me for all those sleepless nights.

About The Author

Renown divorce buster, family counselor, and behavior modification expert, **Patrick T. Hunt M.D.**, practices in Brentwood, California. His innovative techniques coupled with his unique sense of humor have helped couples across America get the magic back in their relationship.

Dr. Hunt, a magna cum laude graduate of the University of Kansas School of Medicine, currently resides in Brentwood California with his wife. The author of many papers, articles, and books, his "Sixty Second Lover Weekend Retreats" have been well attended by couples from all over the world.

TITLES BY CCC PUBLICATIONS

NEW PARTY BOOKS (Available: May 1994)

Retail $4.99

THINGS YOU CAN DO WITH A USELESS MAN

FLYING FUNNIES

MARITAL BLISS & OTHER OXYMORONS

THE VERY VERY SEXY DOT-TO-DOT BOOK

BASTARD'S GUIDE TO BUSINESS SURVIVAL

THE DEFINITIVE FART BOOK

THE TOTAL WIMP'S GUIDE TO SEX

THE CAT OWNER'S SHAPE-UP MANUAL

LIFE'S MOST EMBARRASSING MOMENTS

PMS CRAZED: TOUCH ME & I'LL KILL YOU!

RETIRED: LET THE GAMES BEGIN

MALE BASHING: WOMEN'S FAVORITE PASTIME

THE OFFICE FROM HELL

FOOD & SEX

BUT OSSIFER, IT'S NOT MY FAULT

YOU KNOW YOU'RE AN OLD FART WHEN...

HOW TO REALLY PARTY!!!

HOW TO SURVIVE A JEWISH MOTHER – **Oct.**

1994 NEW TRADE PAPERBACKS – Retail $4.95

SHARING THE ROAD WITH IDIOTS

GREATEST ANSWERING MACHINE MESSAGES

1001 WAYS TO PROCRASTINATE – **May**

FITNESS FANATICS – **Jun.**

THE WORLD'S GREATEST PUT-DOWN LINES – **Jun.**

HORMONES FROM HELL II – **May**

YOUNGER MEN ARE BETTER THAN RETIN-A – **Jul.**

RED HOT MONOGAMY – **($6.95) Jul.**

ROSS PEROT: DON'T QUOTE ME – **Sep.**

BEST SELLING TRADE PAPERBACKS – Retail $4.95
HORMONES FROM HELL ($5.95)
KILLER BRAS & OTHER HAZARDS OF THE 50'S
BETTER TO BE OVER THE HILL THAN UNDER IT
HUSBANDS FROM HELL
HOW TO ENTERTAIN PEOPLE YOU HATE
THE UGLY TRUTH ABOUT MEN
WHAT DO WE DO NOW??
TALK YOUR WAY OUT OF A TRAFFIC TICKET
THE BOTTOM HALF

BEST SELLING TRADE PAPERBACKS – Retail $3.95
NO HANG-UPS
NO HANG-UPS II
NO HANG-UPS III
GETTING EVEN WITH THE ANSWERING MACHINE
NEVER A DULL CARD
WORK SUCKS!
THE PEOPLE WATCHER'S FIELD GUIDE
THE UNOFFICIAL WOMEN'S DIVORCE GUIDE
YOUR GUIDE TO CORPORATE SURVIVAL
THE ABSOLUTE LAST CHANCE DIET BOOK
FOR MEN ONLY (How To Survive Marriage)
SUPERIOR PERSON'S GUIDE TO IRRITATIONS
GIFTING RIGHT
HOW TO GET EVEN WITH YOUR EXes
HOW TO SUCCEED IN SINGLES BARS
OUTRAGEOUS BUMPER-SNICKERS ($2.95)

ACCESSORIES
THE GUILT BAG ($4.95)
THE "MAGIC BOOKMARK" BOOK COVER ($2.95)

NO HANG-UPS – CASSETTES – Retail $4.98
Vol. I: GENERAL MESSAGES
Vol. II: BUSINESS MESSAGES
Vol. III: 'R' RATED MESSAGES
Vol. IV: SOUND EFFECTS ONLY
Vol. V: CELEBRI-TEASE

NOTES: